SQL Made Simple

Bryan Pine

Published by Northwood Lore Books, 2024.

SQL MADE SIMPLE

First edition. November 19, 2024.

ISBN: 979-8230019725

Written by Bryan Pine.

Table of Contents

1. Why Learn SQL? A Day in the Life of Data

Data is everywhere in our modern lives, flowing through countless digital channels and shaping how we work, shop, communicate, and make decisions. Think about your typical morning routine: you check the weather on your phone (data from weather stations), scroll through social media (user interaction data), pay for coffee with a credit card (transaction data), and navigate to work using GPS (location data). By the time you reach your desk, you've already interacted with dozens of databases, each one storing and processing information that makes your daily activities possible. This is why learning SQL, the language of databases, has become as essential as learning to read and write in our data-driven world.

SQL (pronounced "sequel" or "S-Q-L") might sound technical, but at its core, it's simply a way to ask questions about organized information. Imagine you're looking through your email inbox. When you search for messages from a specific person or filter by date, you're essentially performing the same kind of operations that SQL handles with databases. The main difference is that SQL can work with much larger amounts of data and perform more complex operations more quickly than any human could manually.

Let's consider a real-world scenario that many of us face: managing a personal budget. You might currently use a spreadsheet to track your expenses, categorizing purchases and calculating totals for different spending categories. While this works for small amounts of data, imagine if you wanted to analyze years of transactions, identify spending patterns across multiple accounts, or generate detailed reports about your financial habits. This is where SQL shines. With just a few lines of code, you can instantly answer questions like "How much did I spend on groceries in the first quarter compared to last year?" or "What are my top five spending categories on weekends?"

But SQL isn't just for personal use or financial analysis. It's the backbone of virtually every modern business operation. Retail stores use SQL to track inventory and analyze sales patterns. Healthcare providers use it to manage patient records and treatment histories. Marketing teams use it to understand customer behavior and personalize campaigns. Human resources departments use it to manage employee data and payroll. Even your favorite streaming service uses SQL to recommend shows based on viewing history.

The beauty of SQL lies in its intuitive nature. Despite its power, the basic concepts mirror how we naturally think about organizing and retrieving information. When you ask SQL to filter data, it's like sorting through your closet to find all your blue shirts. When you join tables together, it's like combining ingredients from a recipe with cooking instructions. When you group and summarize data, it's like categorizing your monthly expenses into broad categories like "utilities," "entertainment," and "food."

Many people assume that working with databases requires a computer science degree or years of programming experience. This couldn't be further from the truth. While SQL can be used for complex data analysis, its fundamental operations are based on everyday logic. If you can articulate what information you're looking for, you can learn to write SQL queries to find it. The key is starting with familiar concepts and gradually building up to more sophisticated operations.

Throughout this book, we'll take this practical, real-world approach to learning SQL. Instead of memorizing syntax or studying abstract concepts, we'll explore SQL through scenarios you encounter in daily life. Each chapter will present a common situation where data needs to be organized, analyzed, or transformed, and we'll discover how SQL provides elegant solutions to these challenges.

We'll begin with simple queries, like finding specific items in a dataset (similar to searching for a contact in your phone). As your confidence grows, we'll move on to combining information from multiple sources (like planning a party where you need to match guests with dietary preferences and seating arrangements). Eventually, we'll tackle more complex analyses, such as identifying trends over time and making predictions based on historical data.

One of the most valuable aspects of learning SQL is its universal applicability. Unlike many programming languages that may become obsolete or require constant updating, SQL has remained remarkably stable and relevant since its creation in the 1970s. The fundamental concepts you'll learn in this book will serve you well whether you're using a traditional database system like MySQL or PostgreSQL, working with modern cloud platforms, or analyzing big data.

Moreover, SQL skills are highly transferable across industries and roles. Whether you're a business analyst trying to understand market trends, a researcher analyzing experimental data, a marketer tracking campaign performance, or an entrepreneur managing your company's operations, SQL empowers you to work with data effectively and independently. Instead of relying on others to extract and analyze information for you, you can directly access and manipulate the data you need.

As we progress through this book, you'll notice that we focus on practical solutions rather than theoretical perfection. While there are often many ways to write a query to get the same result, we'll emphasize approaches that are clear, efficient, and easy to maintain. You'll learn not just how to write SQL code, but how to think about data problems and break them down into manageable pieces.

We'll also address common challenges and pitfalls you might encounter when working with real-world data. Data is rarely perfect – it can be incomplete, inconsistent, or structured in unexpected ways. You'll learn strategies for handling these situations, from dealing with missing values to cleaning and standardizing information. These practical skills are often more valuable than knowing every possible SQL command.

By the end of this journey, you'll have developed not just technical skills, but a new way of thinking about data. You'll see databases not as intimidating technical constructs, but as powerful tools that can help you understand and analyze the world around you. Whether you're tracking personal finances, managing a small business, or analyzing data for a large corporation, you'll have the skills to work with data confidently and effectively.

Remember, every expert was once a beginner, and every complex query started as a simple question. As we explore SQL together through real-world examples and practical applications, you'll discover that database queries are simply a structured way of asking questions about the information that matters to you. Let's begin this journey into the world of data, where each chapter brings us closer to mastering the art of SQL through the lens of everyday experiences.

2. Setting Up Your First Database: Like Organizing Your Closet

Setting up your first database might sound as technical as assembling a spacecraft, but it's actually more like organizing your closet. Think about the last time you reorganized your wardrobe. You probably sorted clothes by type, color, or season, created designated spaces for different items, and maybe even labeled some storage boxes. Setting up a database follows remarkably similar principles.

Let's start with a simple example that most of us can relate to: creating a database to manage a personal book collection. Just as you might organize your physical bookshelf by genre, author, or publication date, a database provides a structured way to store and organize this information digitally. The first step is choosing the right database management system (DBMS), which is like choosing between different types of storage solutions for your home.

For beginners, SQLite is an excellent choice – it's like a simple storage box that's easy to carry around and requires minimal setup. MySQL and PostgreSQL are more like full-scale closet systems with additional features and capabilities, perfect when you need more organization options. For our purposes, we'll use MySQL as it strikes a good balance between simplicity and functionality.

Installing MySQL is similar to assembling a new shelving unit. Most modern operating systems make this process straightforward – you can download the installer from MySQL's official website, much like picking up a storage system from a furniture store. The installer will guide you through the setup process, asking basic questions like where you want to install the software (which directory on your computer) and what password you'd like to use to protect your data.

Once installed, you'll need to connect to your database server. Think of this as unlocking your storage unit. You can do this through the command line interface (CLI) or using a graphical user interface (GUI) tool like MySQL Workbench. The GUI option is often more comfortable for beginners, just as having a visual organization system is easier than working from memory.

Let's create our first database. In MySQL, this requires a simple command:

```
CREATE DATABASE personal_library;
```

This is like declaring "I'm going to dedicate this space to storing my books." The semicolon at the end is like the period at the end of a sentence – it tells MySQL you've finished your command. After creating the database, you need to tell MySQL you want to use it:

```
USE personal_library;
```

Now comes the interesting part: designing how you'll organize your data. Just as you wouldn't throw all your clothes into a single drawer, you don't want to put all your data into one big table. Instead, you'll create separate tables for different types of information, similar to having different drawers for shirts, pants, and accessories.

For our book collection, we might start with a basic table structure. Creating a table is like setting up a new drawer with specific compartments. Each table needs columns that define what kind of information can go in each "compartment." For example:

```
CREATE TABLE books (
book_id INT PRIMARY KEY AUTO_INCREMENT,
title VARCHAR(255),
author VARCHAR(100),
publication_year INT,
genre VARCHAR(50),
isbn VARCHAR(13),
purchase_date DATE,
price DECIMAL(6,2)
);
```

This structure is similar to creating a spreadsheet, but with more robust rules about what kind of information can go where. The book_id is like a unique label you might put on each item in your closet. VARCHAR(255) means the title can be text up to 255 characters long – like having a space that can fit names of various lengths. The AUTO_INCREMENT feature means MySQL will automatically assign a new number to each book, just as you might number items in your inventory.

Just as you might realize you need additional storage solutions as your wardrobe grows, databases can be modified over time. You can add new columns to existing tables (ALTER TABLE), create new tables for related information, or modify the structure of existing tables to better suit your needs.

Security is another important aspect of database setup. Just as you wouldn't leave your valuable possessions in an unlocked room, you need to protect your database. MySQL's user management system allows you to create different users with various levels of access – similar to giving family members different levels of access to various storage areas in your home.

To create a new user with specific permissions:

CREATE USER 'librarian'@'localhost' IDENTIFIED BY 'password123';

GRANT SELECT, INSERT, UPDATE ON personal_library.* TO 'librarian'@'localhost';

This is like giving someone a key that only opens certain drawers or cabinets. The librarian user can view (SELECT), add (INSERT), and modify (UPDATE) data, but can't delete tables or make structural changes to the database.

As your database grows, you'll want to implement good organizational habits from the start. This includes regular backups (like taking photos of your organized closet for reference), documentation (like keeping a list of what goes where), and maintaining consistent naming conventions (like using clear labels on storage boxes).

Remember that setting up a database is not a one-time task. Just as your storage needs change over time, your database will evolve. You might need to add new tables, modify existing structures, or adjust user permissions. The key is to start with a clear, simple organization system that can grow and adapt as your needs change.

Don't worry if everything doesn't feel perfect right away. Just as it might take several attempts to find the perfect organization system for your closet, you might need to adjust your database structure as you learn more about your data needs. The important thing is to start with a basic structure that works and improve it over time based on how you actually use it.

3. Understanding Tables: Your Digital Filing Cabinet

Understanding tables in a database is much like working with a filing cabinet in your office or home. Imagine walking up to a filing cabinet - each drawer represents a different category of information, and within each drawer, you have folders containing specific documents. In a database, tables work in much the same way, organizing related information into neat, structured collections that are easy to access and manage.

Let's start with a practical example that most people can relate to: organizing a recipe collection. In a physical world, you might have a recipe box with index cards, each containing a recipe's name, ingredients, instructions, cooking time, and serving size. In a database, this becomes a table with columns for each piece of information and rows for each individual recipe.

A table is fundamentally a grid of information, similar to a spreadsheet, but with more rigid rules about what kind of information can go where. Each column in a table has a specific data type that determines what kind of information it can hold. Think of this like having different types of filing folders - some designed for photos, others for legal documents, and still others for receipts. In SQL, common data types include:

INTEGER for whole numbers (like serving sizes or cooking temperatures)

VARCHAR for text of varying length (like recipe names or instructions)

DATE for calendar dates (like when you last made the recipe)

DECIMAL for numbers with decimal points (like ingredient measurements)

BOOLEAN for true/false values (like whether a recipe is vegetarian)

When you create a table, you're essentially setting up the structure for how your data will be organized. Here's how a basic recipe table might be structured in SQL:

```
CREATE TABLE recipes (
recipe_id INTEGER,
recipe_name VARCHAR(100),
preparation_time INTEGER,
cooking_time INTEGER,
serving_size INTEGER,
difficulty_level VARCHAR(20),
is_vegetarian BOOLEAN,
date_added DATE
);
```

Think of this as designing a new index card template for your recipe collection. You're deciding what information you want to track for each recipe and how that information should be formatted. Each row in this table will represent a complete recipe entry, just like each card in your recipe box represents a complete recipe.

One of the most important concepts in table design is the primary key. In our recipe example, recipe_id serves as the primary key - a unique identifier for each recipe. This is similar to how libraries use unique call numbers to identify each book. No two recipes can have the same recipe_id, which helps prevent confusion and ensures we can always find exactly the recipe we're looking for.

Tables also help maintain data integrity through various rules and constraints. For example, you might specify that recipe_name cannot be empty (NULL), or that serving_size must be a positive number. These constraints are like having a friend check your recipe cards to make sure all the necessary information is filled out correctly before filing them away.

Another powerful aspect of tables is their ability to relate to each other. Just as you might have separate sections in your recipe box for main dishes, desserts, and appetizers, databases can have multiple tables that work together. For example, you might have a separate table for ingredients:

```
CREATE TABLE ingredients (
ingredient_id INTEGER,
ingredient_name VARCHAR(50),
unit_of_measure VARCHAR(20),
category VARCHAR(30)
);
```

And another table that connects recipes to their ingredients:

```
CREATE TABLE recipe_ingredients (
recipe_id INTEGER,
ingredient_id INTEGER,
quantity DECIMAL(5,2)
);
```

This relationship between tables is similar to having a cross-reference system in your physical filing cabinet. Instead of writing the same ingredient information over and over on each recipe card, you can simply reference the ingredient list. This not only saves space but also makes it easier to maintain consistency in your data.

When working with tables, it's important to understand how data is actually stored and retrieved. Each row in a table is called a record or tuple, and represents one complete entry. In our recipe example, each row contains all the information about a single recipe. The columns, also called fields or attributes, define what pieces of information we're tracking about each recipe.

Tables also support the concept of indexes, which are like the tabs or dividers in a filing cabinet that help you quickly find what you're looking for. While not visible in the data itself, indexes help databases quickly locate specific records without having to scan through every single row.

Understanding how to properly structure tables is crucial for building efficient databases. This concept is called normalization, and it's similar to organizing your filing cabinet to minimize duplicate information and make updates easier. For example, instead of writing out "tablespoons" hundreds of times in your recipe ingredients, you might create a separate table for units of measurement and just reference them by ID.

As your database grows, you might need to modify your table structure. SQL provides commands to alter existing tables:

ALTER TABLE recipes ADD COLUMN calories INTEGER;

ALTER TABLE recipes DROP COLUMN difficulty_level;

ALTER TABLE recipes MODIFY COLUMN recipe_name VARCHAR(150);

These commands are like reorganizing your filing system - adding new sections, removing unused categories, or changing how information is formatted.

Tables can also include calculated or derived columns, similar to having summary cards in your recipe box that show total preparation time or total calorie count. These can be created using computed columns or views, which we'll explore in later chapters.

Remember that good table design is crucial for building efficient databases. Just as a well-organized filing cabinet makes it easy to find and maintain documents, well-designed database tables make it easy to store, retrieve, and update your data. Take time to plan your table structure carefully, considering what information you need to store and how different pieces of data relate to each other.

When designing tables, always consider the future. Will you need to store additional information later? How might your data requirements change? It's often easier to include additional columns from the start than to add them later when your table contains thousands of records. Think of it like buying a filing cabinet - it's better to have a few empty drawers for future expansion than to run out of space and need to buy a new cabinet.

4. SELECT Statements: Shopping for Exactly What You Need

SELECT statements are the foundation of retrieving information from a database, and they work much like shopping for specific items at a store. Imagine walking into a supermarket with a shopping list. You don't want to look at every single item in the store; you just want to find exactly what you need. That's exactly what SELECT statements do in SQL.

Let's start with a simple example that everyone can relate to. Suppose you have a digital music collection stored in a database table called songs. Just as you might want to look up specific information about your music, like the song title or artist, you can use SELECT to retrieve exactly that information:

SELECT title, artist, album FROM songs;

This is like saying "I want to see the title, artist, and album name for all my songs." The power of SELECT comes from its simplicity and flexibility. You can choose to see all columns in a table by using an asterisk:

SELECT * FROM songs;

However, just like you wouldn't buy everything in a store just because it's there, it's usually better to specify exactly which columns you want. This makes your queries more efficient and your results easier to understand.

Let's explore a more practical scenario: managing a personal book collection. Imagine you have a table called books with columns for title, author, publication_year, genre, and page_count. If you want to see just the titles and authors, you would write:

SELECT title, author FROM books;

The order of columns in your SELECT statement determines the order they appear in your results. This is like arranging items in your shopping cart in a specific way to make them easier to unpack later.

SELECT statements become even more powerful when you start working with multiple tables. Suppose you're managing a small online store, and you want to see information about orders. You might have tables for orders, customers, and products. Just as you might cross reference different shopping lists to plan a party, you can combine information from multiple tables:

SELECT orders.order_date, customers.name, products.product_name

FROM orders, customers, products;

One of the most useful aspects of SELECT statements is their ability to transform data as you retrieve it. Just as you might convert measurements while cooking, you can perform calculations or format data within your SELECT statement. For example, if you're working with a table of expenses:

SELECT description, amount, amount * 1.1 as amount_with_tax FROM expenses;

This calculates the tax-inclusive amount for each expense entry. You can also combine text columns, format numbers, and perform date calculations right in your SELECT statement.

SELECT statements also support aliases, which are like giving temporary nicknames to columns or tables. This is particularly useful when the original column names are long or when you want to make your results more readable:

SELECT first_name || ' ' || last_name AS full_name,

email AS contact_info

FROM customers;

When working with SELECT statements, it's important to understand that they don't modify your data in any way. They simply retrieve and display information, much like looking through a store's window display doesn't actually change the items for sale. This makes SELECT statements safe to experiment with – you can't accidentally delete or modify your data just by looking at it.

You can also use SELECT to retrieve distinct or unique values from a column. This is like making a list of unique categories from your shopping receipts:

```
SELECT DISTINCT genre FROM books;
```

This would show you all the different genres in your book collection, with each genre listed only once, regardless of how many books you have in each category.

SELECT statements can include functions that transform your data as it's being retrieved. For example, you might want to convert text to uppercase or lowercase, round numbers, or format dates:

```
SELECT UPPER(title) as uppercase_title,
ROUND(price, 2) as rounded_price,
DATE_FORMAT(purchase_date, '%M %d, %Y') as formatted_date
FROM purchases;
```

You can also use SELECT to create calculated columns based on multiple fields. For instance, if you're tracking exercise activities:

```
SELECT activity_type,
duration_minutes,
calories_per_minute,
duration_minutes * calories_per_minute as total_calories
FROM workouts;
```

Another powerful feature of SELECT statements is their ability to work with aggregate functions. These are like getting summary information from your shopping receipts:

```
SELECT COUNT(*) as total_books,
AVG(price) as average_price,
MAX(price) as most_expensive,
MIN(price) as least_expensive
```

FROM books;

When working with dates and times, SELECT statements can help you extract specific parts of a timestamp or calculate durations:

```
SELECT event_name,
event_date,
EXTRACT(MONTH FROM event_date) as month,
EXTRACT(YEAR FROM event_date) as year
FROM events;
```

Remember that while SELECT statements can be very powerful, it's important to be specific about what you're requesting. Just as you wouldn't ask a store clerk to show you "everything they have," you should avoid using SELECT * unless you specifically need all columns. This makes your queries more efficient and easier to maintain.

SELECT statements form the foundation for more complex queries we'll explore in later chapters. They're the building blocks for filtering data with WHERE clauses, sorting results with ORDER BY, and combining tables with JOINs. Understanding how to write effective SELECT statements is crucial for working with databases, just as knowing how to make a good shopping list is essential for efficient grocery shopping.

Practice writing SELECT statements with different combinations of columns and functions. Start simple and gradually add more complexity as you become comfortable with the basics. Remember, every complex query starts with a simple SELECT statement, just as every shopping trip starts with a basic shopping list.

5. The WHERE Clause: Sorting Through Your Laundry

Chapter 5 takes us into the world of filtering data using the WHERE clause, a fundamental concept that's as familiar as sorting through your laundry. When you do laundry, you don't wash everything the same way. You separate whites from colors, delicates from heavy items, and maybe even set aside those special care garments. The WHERE clause in SQL works exactly the same way, helping us filter our data based on specific conditions.

Let's start with a simple example that everyone can relate to. Imagine you have a table of clothes in your digital wardrobe. You might want to find all your white shirts, or all the items that need dry cleaning. In SQL, this kind of filtering is handled by the WHERE clause:

SELECT item_name, color, care_instructions FROM wardrobe WHERE color = 'white';

Just as you might sort through your laundry basket to find all your white clothes, this query sorts through your wardrobe table to find all the white items. The WHERE clause always follows the FROM clause and specifies the conditions that must be true for a row to be included in the results.

The real power of the WHERE clause becomes apparent when dealing with numbers. Suppose you're managing your household expenses in a database. You might want to find all transactions over $100:

SELECT transaction_date, description, amount FROM expenses WHERE amount > 100;

This is like going through your receipts and pulling out all the major purchases. The WHERE clause can use various comparison operators: greater than (>), less than (<), equal to (=), and others we'll explore in more detail in the next chapter.

The WHERE clause isn't limited to simple comparisons. You can also search for patterns in text using the LIKE operator. This is similar to looking through your clothes for all items with a certain pattern or brand:

SELECT product_name, brand FROM inventory WHERE brand LIKE 'Nike%';

The % symbol is a wildcard that matches any sequence of characters. This query would find all items where the brand starts with "Nike", whether it's "Nike Air", "Nike Pro", or any other Nike product line.

When working with dates, the WHERE clause becomes particularly useful. Imagine you're looking through your calendar for all events in a particular month:

SELECT event_name, event_date, location FROM events WHERE event_date >= '2023-06-01' AND event_date < '2023-07-01';

This query finds all events in June 2023. It's like flipping through your calendar to the right month and listing all the appointments and events you have scheduled.

The WHERE clause can also check for multiple conditions using AND and OR operators. This is similar to sorting laundry with multiple criteria. For instance, you might want to find all white or light-colored delicate items:

SELECT item_name, color, fabric_type FROM wardrobe WHERE (color = 'white' OR color = 'light blue') AND care_type = 'delicate';

You can also use the WHERE clause to find items that match values in a list, using the IN operator. This is like checking items against a shopping list:

SELECT product_name, price FROM products WHERE category IN ('Electronics', 'Appliances', 'Computers');

One particularly useful feature of the WHERE clause is its ability to find items that fall within a range using the BETWEEN operator. This is similar to sorting clothes by size range:

SELECT item_name, size FROM clothing WHERE size BETWEEN 'M' AND 'XL';

The WHERE clause can also help you find missing or incomplete information using the IS NULL operator. This is like finding all the socks without matches:

SELECT item_name, last_seen_date FROM items WHERE matching_item IS NULL;

When working with text data, the WHERE clause allows for case-sensitive or case-insensitive comparisons, depending on your database settings. You might want to find all items regardless of how the brand name is capitalized:

SELECT product_name FROM inventory WHERE LOWER(brand) = 'nike';

The WHERE clause becomes even more powerful when combined with functions. For example, you might want to find all transactions from the current month:

SELECT transaction_date, amount FROM expenses WHERE MONTH(transaction_date) = MONTH(CURRENT_DATE);

Remember that the WHERE clause filters rows before any grouping or aggregation occurs. This is like sorting your laundry before deciding how many loads you need to do. The order of operations is important because it affects your final results.

You can also use the WHERE clause with subqueries, which are like creating a temporary sorting rule. For example, finding all products more expensive than the average price:

SELECT product_name, price FROM products WHERE price > (SELECT AVG(price) FROM products);

When using the WHERE clause, it's important to consider performance. Just as it's more efficient to sort laundry once rather than searching through the whole pile for each type of item, well-structured WHERE clauses can make your queries run faster.

The WHERE clause is often used in combination with other SQL features we'll explore in later chapters. You might want to filter data before sorting it (WHERE with ORDER BY), or before grouping it (WHERE with GROUP BY). Understanding how to effectively use the WHERE clause is crucial for working with databases, just as knowing how to properly sort laundry is essential for effective cleaning.

As you practice writing queries with WHERE clauses, start with simple conditions and gradually add complexity. Remember that every complex filter starts with a basic condition, just as every laundry sorting task starts with a simple separation of lights and darks. The key is to think about your data like you think about everyday sorting tasks – what criteria do you use to separate items, and how can you express those criteria in SQL?

6. Comparison Operators: Making Daily Decisions

Imagine making decisions in your daily life. When you wake up in the morning, you might check the temperature to decide what to wear. If it's below 60 degrees, you'll grab a jacket. If it's above 80 degrees, you'll opt for shorts. These simple "if-then" decisions are exactly how comparison operators work in SQL, and they're essential tools for filtering data in meaningful ways.

In SQL, comparison operators help us make these yes-or-no decisions about our data. Just like you might say "I want all shirts that cost less than $30" when shopping, you can use SQL to find all products in a database that meet specific criteria. The basic comparison operators in SQL are probably familiar to you from math class: equal to (=), greater than (>), less than (<), greater than or equal to (>=), less than or equal to (<=), and not equal to (<>).

Let's start with a practical example that many of us face: managing a household budget. Imagine you have a table called expenses that tracks your monthly spending. You want to find all purchases that cost more than $100. In SQL, you'd write: SELECT * FROM expenses WHERE amount > 100. This is just like going through your receipts and pulling out all the big ticket items. The comparison operator > tells SQL to only show expenses that are more than $100.

But what if you want to find all expenses that are exactly $50? That's where the equals operator (=) comes in handy. SELECT * FROM expenses WHERE amount = 50 will find those precise matches. Think of it like searching for a specific shirt size you're looking for at a store you don't want medium or large, you want exactly small.

The less than (<) and greater than (>) operators are particularly useful when dealing with dates. Suppose you're managing an events calendar and want to find all upcoming events. You might write:

SELECT * FROM events WHERE event_date > '2024-01-01'. This works just like looking at your wall calendar and focusing only on dates after New Year's Day.

One common scenario where comparison operators shine is in inventory management. Let's say you run a small bookstore and need to know which books are running low on stock. You might use the less than or equal to operator (<=) like this: SELECT book_title, stock_quantity FROM books WHERE stock_quantity <= 5. This query helps you identify books that need reordering, just like checking your pantry shelves to see which items are running low.

The not equal to operator (<>) is particularly useful when you want to exclude certain items. Maybe you're planning meals for the week but want to avoid chicken. You could write: SELECT * FROM recipes WHERE main_ingredient <> 'chicken'. This works just like flipping through a cookbook and skipping past all the chicken recipes.

Sometimes you need to find values within a range, and that's where combining comparison operators becomes powerful. Suppose you're looking for products priced between $10 and $20. You can write: SELECT * FROM products WHERE price >= 10 AND price <= 20. This is similar to shopping with a budget range in mind you're not interested in items that are too cheap or too expensive.

When working with text data, comparison operators can help with alphabetical ordering. For example, if you want to find all customers whose last names come after 'M' in the alphabet, you'd write: SELECT * FROM customers WHERE last_name > 'M'. This works just like organizing books on a shelf or filing papers alphabetically.

One common gotcha with comparison operators involves comparing NULL values. NULL represents missing or unknown data, and it behaves differently from other values. You can't use regular comparison operators with NULL. Instead, you need to use special operators IS NULL or IS NOT NULL. For example, if you want to find all phone numbers that haven't been provided in your contacts list, you'd write: SELECT * FROM contacts WHERE phone_number IS NULL.

Another important consideration when using comparison operators is data type matching. Just like you wouldn't compare apples to oranges, SQL needs to compare similar types of data. If you're comparing numbers, both values should be numbers. If you're comparing dates, both values should be dates. Mixing data types can lead to unexpected results or errors.

Comparison operators also work with subqueries, which are queries nested inside other queries. For example, if you want to find all products that cost more than the average price, you could write: SELECT * FROM products WHERE price > (SELECT AVG(price) FROM products). This is like first calculating the average price of all items in a store, then walking around and noting which items cost more than that average.

When dealing with text comparisons, be aware that they are usually case sensitive depending on your database settings. This means 'SMITH' and 'Smith' might be treated as different values. Many databases provide case insensitive comparison functions if you need them.

Performance wise, comparison operators are very efficient, especially when used with indexed columns. Think of an index like the tabs in a phone book that help you quickly find names starting with certain letters. Without an index, the database has to check every single row to make comparisons, like flipping through every page of a book to find something.

A practical tip when using comparison operators is to always validate your assumptions. If you're not getting the results you expect, double check your operator and your values. Sometimes a simple typo like using < instead of > can completely change your results. It's like double checking whether you want items less than $50 or more than $50 before filtering your shopping options.

Remember that comparison operators can be combined with other SQL features we'll learn about later, like JOINs and aggregate functions. This allows for powerful queries that can answer complex questions about your data. For instance, you might want to find all customers who have spent more than the average order amount, which combines comparison operators with grouping and aggregation.

In real world applications, comparison operators are often used in dynamic queries where the values come from user input or application variables. For example, a web application might let users filter products by price range, using comparison operators behind the scenes to show the right items.

As you continue working with SQL, you'll find that mastering comparison operators is crucial for effective data filtering. They're the building blocks for more complex queries and data analysis tasks. Just remember: if you can make a yes or no decision about something in real life, you can probably use a comparison operator to make the same decision about your data in SQL.

7. Multiple Conditions: Planning a Party Guest List

Let's explore how SQL handles multiple conditions by thinking about planning a party guest list. When you're organizing a party, you often need to consider multiple factors simultaneously. Should you invite your college friends and your work colleagues? What about people who live more than 50 miles away but are close family members? These kinds of multi-layered decisions are exactly what we handle in SQL using logical operators AND, OR, and NOT.

Think about how you make party planning decisions in real life. You might say "I want to invite people who are either family members OR close friends." In SQL, this translates directly using the OR operator. For example: SELECT * FROM contacts WHERE relationship = 'family' OR relationship = 'close friend'. This works just like sorting through your address book and creating two piles one for family and one for friends and then combining them into your invitation list.

The AND operator helps us when we need all conditions to be true, like finding guests who both drink coffee AND live locally for a morning coffee gathering. In SQL, this might look like: SELECT * FROM contacts WHERE drinks_coffee = 'yes' AND distance_miles < 20. This is similar to taking your initial guest list and narrowing it down based on multiple preferences just as you might exclude people who don't drink coffee or live too far away.

Real world scenarios often require combining AND and OR operators. Suppose you're planning a child's birthday party and want to invite either classmates who are in the same grade OR neighborhood kids who are within two years of age. In SQL, you might write: SELECT * FROM kids_contacts WHERE (school_grade = 5 AND class = 'A') OR (neighborhood = 'Oak Street' AND ABS(age - 10) <=

2). Notice how we use parentheses to group conditions together, just like you might mentally group your decision criteria when thinking through who to invite.

The NOT operator comes in handy when you want to exclude certain combinations. Maybe you don't want to invite people who are both from work AND live more than 30 miles away since they might be too tired after their commute. You could write: SELECT * FROM contacts WHERE NOT (workplace = 'office' AND distance_miles > 30). This is like going through your guest list and removing people who meet both of these criteria.

One common scenario is finding people who meet one set of criteria but not another. For instance, you might want to invite friends who like dancing but haven't attended your last three parties. The query might look like: SELECT * FROM friends WHERE likes_dancing = 'yes' AND NOT EXISTS (SELECT * FROM past_parties WHERE past_parties.friend_id = friends.id AND party_date >= DATE_SUB(CURRENT_DATE, INTERVAL 3 MONTH)). This combines multiple conditions with subqueries to create a more refined selection.

When working with multiple conditions, it's important to understand how SQL evaluates them. Just like in mathematics, SQL follows an order of operations. AND is processed before OR, which is why proper parentheses are crucial. Consider the difference between these two queries: SELECT * FROM guests WHERE age > 21 OR age < 12 AND guardian_present = 'yes' versus SELECT * FROM guests WHERE (age > 21 OR age < 12) AND guardian_present = 'yes'. The placement of parentheses completely changes who gets selected.

Complex conditions often involve comparing multiple columns to multiple values. Suppose you're organizing a dinner party and need to accommodate dietary restrictions. You might write: SELECT * FROM friends WHERE dietary_preference IN ('vegan', 'vegetarian') AND allergies NOT LIKE '%nut%' AND (alcohol_preference = 'wine' OR alcohol_preference = 'none'). This query helps you plan a menu that works for everyone, just like you would consider multiple dietary needs when planning in real life.

Error handling becomes particularly important when dealing with multiple conditions. What happens if some of your data is missing? For example, if you're checking both email and phone number preferences for party invitations, you might write: SELECT * FROM contacts WHERE (email_preference = 'yes' OR email_preference IS NULL) AND (phone_preference = 'yes' OR phone_preference IS NULL). This handles cases where contact preferences haven't been recorded, preventing potential guests from being accidentally excluded.

Performance considerations come into play when using multiple conditions. Just like you might organize your physical address book for quicker searching, databases use indexes to speed up queries. However, complex conditions can make it harder for the database to use these indexes effectively. It's often helpful to structure your conditions in a way that takes advantage of indexed columns first.

A practical tip when working with multiple conditions is to build them up gradually. Start with a simple condition and test it, then add more conditions one at a time. This makes it easier to understand exactly how each condition affects your results and helps prevent logical errors. It's like starting with a basic guest list and carefully adding criteria rather than trying to apply all your filtering rules at once.

Remember that conditions can also include calculations or functions. Maybe you want to invite people whose birthday falls within the next month and who have attended at least 50% of your past events. The query might look like: SELECT * FROM friends WHERE DATEDIFF(birthday, CURRENT_DATE) BETWEEN 0 AND 30 AND (attended_events * 100 / total_events) >= 50. This combines date functions, mathematical calculations, and multiple conditions to create sophisticated selection criteria.

As you work with multiple conditions, you'll develop an intuition for how to structure them effectively. The key is to think about your real world decision making process and translate that logic into SQL. Just as you naturally combine different factors when making decisions about your party guest list, SQL gives you the tools to express these complex criteria in a clear and organized way.

8. Working with Text: Managing Your Contact List

Working with text in SQL is much like managing your personal contact list. Just as you might need to find someone's phone number, update an address, or search for all contacts whose names start with "J," SQL provides powerful tools for handling text data, often called strings.

Let's start with a common scenario: searching for a contact by name. In your phone, you might start typing "Jo" and see all contacts whose names begin with those letters. In SQL, we use the LIKE operator with a wildcard for this kind of pattern matching. For example, SELECT * FROM contacts WHERE first_name LIKE 'Jo%' would find people named John, Joseph, and Joanna. The percent sign (%) acts as a wildcard, matching any number of characters that might follow.

Sometimes you need to be more specific in your search. Maybe you remember that someone's name has "ann" in it, but you're not sure if it's at the beginning, middle, or end. You can use wildcards on both sides: SELECT * FROM contacts WHERE first_name LIKE '%ann%' would find names like Anna, Joanna, and Suzanne. This is similar to using the search function in your phone's contacts app to find a name when you only remember part of it.

Managing text often involves cleaning up inconsistent data. Think about how annoying it is when some contacts are stored with all capital letters while others use proper capitalization. SQL provides functions like UPPER(), LOWER(), and INITCAP() (in some databases) to standardize text. If you wanted to standardize all email addresses to lowercase, you might use: UPDATE contacts SET email = LOWER(email). This ensures consistency, just like you might standardize how you write addresses in your personal address book.

Text concatenation is another common need. Perhaps you want to combine first and last names into a full name, or join an address's components into a single line. The concatenation operator (usually || or +, depending on your database) helps here: SELECT first_name || ' ' || last_name AS full_name FROM contacts. Some databases also offer the CONCAT() function for this purpose. This is like when you're creating mailing labels and need to combine different pieces of contact information into a single, properly formatted string.

Often, you need to clean up unnecessary spaces in text data. Just as you might fix extra spaces in a written address, SQL provides the TRIM() function to remove unwanted spaces from the beginning and end of text. LTRIM() and RTRIM() handle spaces on just the left or right side. For example, UPDATE contacts SET phone_number = TRIM(phone_number) removes any accidental spaces that might have been entered around phone numbers.

Working with portions of text is another common task. Maybe you need just the first three letters of each last name for creating user IDs. The SUBSTRING() or SUBSTR() function (name varies by database) lets you extract parts of text: SELECT SUBSTRING(last_name, 1, 3) FROM contacts. This is similar to how you might abbreviate names when making quick notes in your address book.

Text replacement is useful when you need to standardize data. Suppose some phone numbers use dots while others use dashes. The REPLACE() function helps maintain consistency: UPDATE contacts SET phone = REPLACE(phone, '.', '-'). This is like going through your contact list and making sure all phone numbers follow the same format.

Length checks are important for data validation. You might want to find all phone numbers that don't match the expected length: SELECT * FROM contacts WHERE LENGTH(phone_number) != 10. This helps identify potentially incorrect entries, just as you might spot a phone number that looks too short or too long in your paper address book.

Position finding helps locate specific characters within text. Perhaps you need to find email addresses that don't contain an @ symbol: SELECT * FROM contacts WHERE POSITION('@' IN email) = 0. This is similar to quickly scanning addresses to make sure they look valid.

String functions can be combined for more complex operations. Maybe you want to create username suggestions based on the first letter of the first name and up to seven letters of the last name: SELECT LOWER(CONCAT(SUBSTRING(first_name, 1, 1), SUBSTRING(last_name, 1, 7))) AS username FROM contacts. This combines multiple text operations just as you might follow a specific rule when creating nicknames for contacts.

Regular expressions provide even more powerful pattern matching capabilities, though support varies by database. They're like having a super-powered search function that can find complex patterns in text. For example, finding all phone numbers that match a specific format or email addresses that end in certain domains.

When working with international contacts, character set handling becomes important. Different databases handle special characters and accents differently. It's like making sure you can properly record names with accents or characters from different alphabets in your contact list.

Text comparison requires careful consideration of case sensitivity. Some databases treat 'Smith' and 'SMITH' as different values by default, while others consider them the same. You can control this behavior with functions like UPPER() or LOWER() in your comparisons: WHERE UPPER(last_name) = 'SMITH'.

Performance considerations come into play when working with text operations. Just as it's slower to scan through a long contact list looking for partial matches versus exact names, text pattern matching with LIKE and regular expressions can be slower than exact matching. Proper indexing strategies become important for frequently searched text columns.

Error handling is crucial when working with text. What happens if data contains unexpected characters or doesn't match expected patterns? Defensive programming techniques, like checking text length and format before processing, help prevent errors. This is similar to verifying information when taking down contact details to ensure accuracy.

Remember that text operations can be resource-intensive, especially with large datasets. It's often more efficient to process text data when inserting or updating records rather than transforming it repeatedly during queries. Think of this as organizing your contacts properly from the start rather than having to fix formatting issues later.

9. Basic Math in SQL: Balancing Your Checkbook

Just as we balance our checkbooks and track our expenses, SQL provides powerful tools for performing mathematical calculations on our data. Let's explore how SQL handles basic arithmetic operations through the lens of personal finance management.

Imagine you're reviewing your monthly expenses and need to calculate various totals and averages. SQL supports all the basic arithmetic operators you'd use with a calculator: addition (+), subtraction (-), multiplication (*), and division (/). For example, if you want to calculate the total cost of all purchases including tax, you might write: SELECT price + (price * tax_rate) AS total_cost FROM purchases. This is just like adding sales tax to your receipt totals.

When working with money, precision is crucial. You wouldn't want rounding errors in your bank balance! SQL handles decimal numbers (often called numeric or decimal types) with specific precision. Think of it like balancing your checkbook to the penny. When you write SELECT price * quantity AS subtotal FROM orders, SQL maintains proper decimal places in the calculation, just as you would when multiplying an item's cost by the quantity purchased.

Calculating averages is a common need in financial analysis. Perhaps you want to know your average daily spending for the month. The AVG() function in SQL handles this naturally: SELECT AVG(amount) FROM expenses WHERE MONTH(date) = 6. This is similar to adding up all your expenses and dividing by the number of days, but SQL does the heavy lifting for you.

Sometimes you need to round numbers to make them more manageable. Just as you might round to the nearest dollar when estimating expenses, SQL's ROUND() function helps format numbers: SELECT ROUND(amount, 2) FROM transactions ensures values show exactly two decimal places. Some databases also offer CEILING() and FLOOR() functions for rounding up or down to the nearest whole number, useful for conservative or liberal estimates.

Percentage calculations are essential for budget analysis. If you want to see what percentage of your income goes to different expense categories, you might write: SELECT category, (amount / total_income) * 100 AS percentage FROM expenses. This mirrors the mental math you do when figuring out if you're spending too much on dining out or entertainment.

Running totals help track cumulative spending. While more complex in pure SQL, you can calculate running balances with window functions: SELECT date, amount, SUM(amount) OVER (ORDER BY date) AS running_total FROM transactions. This is like maintaining a running balance in your checkbook, where each entry adds to or subtracts from the previous total.

Mathematical functions in SQL extend beyond basic arithmetic. The ABS() function returns absolute values, useful when you're interested in the size of a transaction regardless of whether it's a credit or debit. POWER() and SQRT() handle exponential calculations, which might come into play when calculating compound interest or investment growth.

When working with percentages, you often need to convert between decimal and percentage formats. Multiplying by 100 converts a decimal to a percentage, while dividing by 100 does the reverse. SELECT discount_rate * 100 AS discount_percentage FROM sales shows discount rates in a more readable percentage format.

Null values require special consideration in mathematical operations. Just as a missing receipt entry throws off your balance, any calculation involving NULL in SQL results in NULL. The COALESCE() function helps handle these cases by providing a default value: SELECT COALESCE(amount, 0) + tax AS total ensures your calculations continue even with missing values.

Integer division might surprise you if you're not careful. In many SQL databases, dividing two integers returns an integer result, truncating any decimal portion. To get decimal results, ensure at least one operand is a decimal number. SELECT 5.0 / 2 returns 2.5, while SELECT 5 / 2 might return 2, depending on your database.

Aggregating numerical data often involves multiple calculations. For example, to analyze your spending patterns, you might need totals, averages, minimums, and maximums all at once: SELECT category, SUM(amount) AS total, AVG(amount) AS average, MIN(amount) AS minimum, MAX(amount) AS maximum FROM expenses GROUP BY category. This gives you a comprehensive view of your spending habits.

Currency conversion calculations are common in financial applications. If you're tracking expenses in multiple currencies, you might write: SELECT amount * exchange_rate AS converted_amount FROM transactions. This is similar to converting prices when traveling internationally.

Mathematical operations can be combined with conditional logic. Perhaps you want to apply different discount rates based on purchase amounts. The CASE statement helps here: SELECT amount * CASE WHEN amount > 1000 THEN 0.9 WHEN amount > 500 THEN 0.95 ELSE 1 END AS discounted_amount FROM orders.

Performance considerations come into play with mathematical operations, especially when processing large datasets. Just as you might use a spreadsheet for complex calculations instead of doing them by hand, indexes and optimized query structures help SQL perform calculations efficiently.

Remember that different database systems might handle mathematical operations slightly differently, especially regarding precision and rounding. Always test calculations with sample data to ensure they behave as expected. This is like double checking your math when balancing your checkbook – it's better to catch errors early than deal with their consequences later.

When dealing with financial calculations, it's crucial to understand how your database handles numeric precision. Using the appropriate data types (DECIMAL or NUMERIC rather than FLOAT) ensures accuracy in monetary calculations, just as you would never use rough estimates when managing real money.

10. ORDER BY: Arranging Books on a Shelf

Think of arranging data in SQL like organizing books on a shelf. Just as you might arrange books by author's last name, publication date, or genre, SQL's ORDER BY clause lets you sort your data in meaningful ways.

When working with data, having information in a random order is like having a messy bookshelf where nothing is where you expect it. The ORDER BY clause brings order to chaos, allowing us to arrange our results in ways that make them easier to understand and analyze.

Let's start with the basics. A simple ORDER BY statement works just like alphabetizing books. If you have a table of books, writing SELECT title FROM books ORDER BY title arranges all the titles alphabetically, from A to Z. This is the default ascending order, just like how you learned the alphabet. If you want to reverse the order, like arranging books from Z to A, you add the DESC keyword: SELECT title FROM books ORDER BY title DESC.

But sorting doesn't have to be limited to text. Just as you might arrange books by publication date to see the newest releases first, you can sort any type of data. Numbers, dates, and even custom data types can all be arranged logically. SELECT product_name, price FROM products ORDER BY price puts your items in order from least to most expensive.

One powerful feature of ORDER BY is the ability to sort by multiple columns, like organizing books first by genre, then by author within each genre. For example, SELECT first_name, last_name, birth_date FROM customers ORDER BY last_name, first_name sorts your customer list by last name and then by first name for customers sharing the same last name.

Sometimes you might want different sorting directions for different columns. Just as you might arrange history books chronologically but their subsections alphabetically, you can mix ascending and descending sorts: SELECT product_name, stock_level, price FROM products ORDER BY stock_level DESC, price ASC shows items with highest stock first, and within each stock level, orders by price from lowest to highest.

The ORDER BY clause always comes at the end of your query, after any WHERE, GROUP BY, or HAVING clauses. This makes sense when you think about it – you want to filter and group your data before deciding how to arrange it, just like you would sort books into genres before alphabetizing within each section.

Sorting can also work with calculated columns. Imagine arranging books by their price-to-page ratio to find the best value. You might write SELECT title, price, pages, price/pages AS price_per_page FROM books ORDER BY price_per_page. The ORDER BY clause can reference any column in your SELECT list, including calculated values.

NULL values require special consideration in sorting. By default, NULL values are treated as the lowest possible values in ascending order and highest in descending order. This is like having a special shelf for books you haven't yet categorized. You can control NULL positioning using NULLS FIRST or NULLS LAST in databases that support these clauses.

When dealing with text sorting, be aware of case sensitivity. Some databases treat uppercase and lowercase letters differently when sorting, while others don't. It's like deciding whether "The Great Gatsby" should come before or after "the hobbit." You can use functions like UPPER() or LOWER() in your ORDER BY clause to ensure consistent sorting: ORDER BY LOWER(title).

Performance considerations come into play with sorting, especially for large datasets. Creating indexes on commonly sorted columns is like having a card catalog in a library – it makes finding and ordering information much faster. Without proper indexes, sorting large datasets can be like manually checking every book on every shelf.

You can also sort by column position rather than column name, though this isn't recommended for production code. SELECT title, author, year FROM books ORDER BY 3 sorts by the year column (the third column in the SELECT list). While this might save some typing, it makes your queries harder to maintain, like trying to find a book when someone has rearranged your shelving system.

Some databases support more advanced sorting options. For example, you might want to sort strings naturally, so that "Book 2" comes before "Book 10" instead of following standard ASCII sorting where "10" comes before "2". Many databases offer special functions for these cases.

Remember that sorting happens after most other query operations. This means you can sort aggregated data, filtered results, or joined tables. It's like being able to organize books after you've already selected only certain genres or only books published by specific publishers.

The ORDER BY clause is one of SQL's most frequently used features because organized data is simply more useful. Whether you're presenting information to users, preparing reports, or analyzing trends, having data in a logical order makes it easier to understand and work with, just like a well-organized bookshelf makes finding your favorite book a breeze.

11. Managing Dates: Planning Your Calendar

Managing dates in SQL is like keeping track of events in your calendar. Just as you record birthdays, appointments, and deadlines, databases need to handle all sorts of date-related information efficiently and accurately.

Think about how you use dates in your daily life. You might need to know how many days until your next appointment, find all events happening next month, or calculate how long you've been at your current job. SQL provides powerful tools for handling all these date-related tasks and more.

Let's start with the basics of storing dates. Different database systems might format dates slightly differently, but they all follow similar principles. Just as you might write a date as "December 25, 2023" or "2023-12-25", SQL databases have standardized ways to store and display dates. The most common format is 'YYYY-MM-DD', which avoids any ambiguity about whether 12/01/2023 means January 12th or December 1st.

Working with dates often involves comparing them, just like checking if your dentist appointment is before or after your lunch meeting. SQL makes these comparisons straightforward: SELECT * FROM appointments WHERE appointment_date > '2023-12-01' finds all appointments after December 1st, 2023. You can use the same comparison operators (<, >, =, <=, >=) that you use with numbers.

One of the most common date operations is finding the current date. Just as you might need to know today's date to plan your schedule, SQL provides functions like CURRENT_DATE or GETDATE() (depending on your database system). This is incredibly useful for tasks like finding upcoming events: SELECT * FROM events WHERE event_date >= CURRENT_DATE ORDER BY event_date shows all future events in chronological order.

Date arithmetic is another powerful feature. Need to find all orders from the last 30 days? Just as you might count back days on your calendar, SQL lets you add or subtract days, months, or years from dates. The exact syntax varies by database, but the concept is universal. For example, SELECT * FROM orders WHERE order_date >= CURRENT_DATE - INTERVAL '30' DAY finds recent orders.

Extracting parts of dates is like breaking down your calendar into more manageable pieces. Just as you might want to see all events in July regardless of the year, SQL lets you pull out specific components of dates. Functions like EXTRACT, YEAR, MONTH, and DAY let you work with just the parts you need. SELECT EXTRACT(MONTH FROM birth_date) AS birth_month FROM employees groups birthdays by month.

Formatting dates for display is another important aspect. Just as you might write dates differently for different audiences (formal letters versus casual notes), SQL provides functions to format dates in various ways. Functions like TO_CHAR or DATE_FORMAT let you convert dates into readable strings: "Monday, December 25, 2023" instead of "2023-12-25".

Date ranges are particularly useful for reporting and analysis. Imagine checking your calendar for all events between two dates. SQL handles this naturally with BETWEEN: SELECT * FROM meetings WHERE meeting_date BETWEEN '2023-01-01' AND '2023-12-31' finds all meetings in 2023.

Working with timestamps adds another layer of precision, including hours, minutes, and seconds. This is like having a detailed schedule that tracks not just the day of your appointments, but the exact time. Timestamps can include timezone information too, crucial for coordinating across different regions.

Calculating durations between dates is another common task. Just as you might need to know how many days until your vacation or how long a project took to complete, SQL provides functions to find the difference between dates. DATEDIFF or similar functions return the number of days, months, or years between two dates.

Date manipulation becomes particularly powerful when combined with other SQL features. You might GROUP BY month to see patterns in your data, JOIN tables based on date ranges, or use window functions to analyze trends over time. These combinations let you answer complex questions about your data's temporal aspects.

Remember to handle date formats carefully when inserting or updating data. Just as writing the wrong date in your calendar can cause confusion, incorrect date formats can lead to errors or incorrect results. Most databases will convert string representations of dates automatically, but it's best to be explicit about your date formats to avoid any ambiguity.

Time zones can add complexity to date handling, just like coordinating meetings across different regions. Many databases store dates in UTC (Coordinated Universal Time) and convert them to local time zones as needed. This ensures consistency regardless of where your users are located.

Finally, don't forget about leap years and other calendar complexities. Just as your wall calendar accounts for these special cases, SQL's date functions handle them automatically. You don't need to worry about whether February has 28 or 29 days – the database takes care of these details for you.

12. DISTINCT: Finding Unique Items in Your Grocery List

Think about the last time you went grocery shopping with a list that had accidentally listed "milk" three times. You only needed one entry for milk, not three! This is exactly the kind of situation where SQL's DISTINCT keyword comes in handy. It helps us find unique items in our data, removing duplicates just like you would clean up that grocery list.

DISTINCT is one of SQL's simpler yet powerful features. Imagine you want to know which countries your customers come from. Without DISTINCT, if you have 1000 customers and 100 are from Canada, 200 from Mexico, and 700 from the United States, a simple SELECT country FROM customers would show you all 1000 rows, with countries repeated many times. But SELECT DISTINCT country FROM customers shows you just three rows: Canada, Mexico, and United States.

The real power of DISTINCT becomes apparent when you start thinking about real world scenarios. Consider a retail database tracking product sales. You might want to know which products have ever been sold, regardless of how many times each has been purchased. Instead of seeing the same product listed multiple times for each sale, SELECT DISTINCT product_name FROM sales gives you a clean list of unique products.

DISTINCT can work with multiple columns too, which is particularly useful when you need unique combinations of values. Let's say you're planning a series of training sessions and want to know all the unique instructor-course combinations that have ever been scheduled. SELECT DISTINCT instructor_name, course_name FROM training_sessions shows you each unique pairing, helping you understand your teaching patterns.

One common misconception about DISTINCT is that it only works with text. In reality, it works with any data type, including numbers, dates, and even combinations of different types. For example, if you're analyzing customer behavior, you might use SELECT DISTINCT customer_id, purchase_date FROM orders to see the unique days when each customer made purchases.

The performance impact of DISTINCT is worth considering. Just as it would take longer to manually review a long list to remove duplicates than to read through it once, DISTINCT requires additional processing time. The database needs to compare each row with every other row to identify duplicates. For small datasets, this isn't a concern, but for large tables, you might want to consider whether you really need distinct values.

DISTINCT becomes particularly powerful when combined with other SQL features. For instance, you might use it inside a subquery: SELECT * FROM customers WHERE country IN (SELECT DISTINCT country FROM orders) finds all customers from countries where orders have been placed. Or you might combine it with COUNT to find out how many unique values exist: SELECT COUNT(DISTINCT status) FROM orders tells you how many different order statuses are in use.

Sometimes you'll encounter situations where you need distinct values from some columns but want to see associated data from other columns. This is where things can get tricky. You can't simply add more columns to a DISTINCT query and expect meaningful results. Instead, you might need to use subqueries or window functions to achieve your goal.

A practical example helps illustrate this: imagine you're analyzing sales data and want to know the first sale date for each unique product. You might write something like: SELECT DISTINCT product_name, MIN(sale_date) OVER (PARTITION BY product_name) as first_sale FROM sales. This gives you each product exactly once, along with its earliest sale date.

DISTINCT NULL handling is another important consideration. In SQL, NULL represents missing or unknown values, and DISTINCT treats NULL values as equal to each other. If you have multiple rows where a column contains NULL, DISTINCT will return just one NULL. This can be exactly what you want – or it might surprise you if you're not expecting it.

When working with DISTINCT, it's helpful to think about whether you really need it. Sometimes, other SQL features might be more appropriate. For instance, if you're trying to count unique values, COUNT(DISTINCT column_name) is often more efficient than counting the results of a SELECT DISTINCT query. Similarly, if you're looking for unique combinations of values, GROUP BY might be more appropriate and often performs better.

DISTINCT can also be useful for data quality checks. If you're expecting certain columns to contain unique values (like employee IDs or product codes), comparing the count of all rows to the count of distinct values can quickly identify duplicate entries that might indicate data problems.

Remember that DISTINCT operates on rows, not individual values. If you SELECT DISTINCT first_name, last_name FROM customers, you'll get unique combinations of first and last names. This means if you have two different John Smiths, they'll appear as one row, which might not be what you want. In such cases, you'd need to include additional identifying columns in your DISTINCT clause.

As with many SQL features, the key to using DISTINCT effectively is understanding exactly what you're trying to achieve. Are you looking for unique values, or do you actually need to group and count? Do you need distinct combinations of multiple columns, or just unique values in one column? Answering these questions will help you write more efficient and accurate queries.

13. NULL Values: Dealing with Missing Information

Let's explore how databases handle missing information, something we encounter constantly in our daily lives. Think about your address book - some contacts might be missing phone numbers, others might not have email addresses listed. Or consider a recipe box where some recipe cards are missing cooking temperatures or prep times. These gaps in our information are represented in SQL using NULL values.

NULL is a special marker that indicates missing or unknown information. It's different from zero, an empty string, or blank space. When your friend hasn't told you their new address yet, you wouldn't write "0" or leave a blank - you'd mark it as unknown. That's exactly what NULL does in a database.

Understanding NULL values is crucial because they behave differently from other values in SQL. You can't compare NULL using normal comparison operators like = or <>. If you try WHERE phone_number = NULL, you won't get the results you expect. Instead, you need to use special operators: IS NULL and IS NOT NULL. It's like asking "Do I know this person's phone number?" rather than "What is this person's phone number?"

Let's consider a practical example. Imagine you're managing a library database and want to find all books that don't have a return date recorded. You'd write WHERE return_date IS NULL rather than WHERE return_date = NULL. This seemingly small distinction is important - it's the difference between finding missing information and finding nothing at all.

NULL values can create unexpected results in calculations too. If you're calculating the average order value in a sales database, any NULL prices will be excluded from the calculation entirely. This makes sense when you think about it - if you're calculating your monthly expenses and some receipts are missing, you can't include those unknown amounts in your total.

When working with NULL values, it's helpful to use the COALESCE function. COALESCE lets you specify a default value to use when you encounter a NULL. Think of it like leaving notes for yourself: "If I don't know the phone number, use 'Contact needed'" or "If the price isn't recorded, use 0." In SQL, you might write COALESCE(phone_number, 'Contact needed') or COALESCE(price, 0).

NULL values become particularly interesting when you're joining tables. In a LEFT JOIN, if there's no matching record in the right table, you'll get NULL values for all columns from that table. This can be useful for finding gaps in your data - like identifying customers who have never placed an order or products that have never been reviewed.

Another common scenario involving NULL values is form submissions. When customers fill out online forms, they might skip optional fields. These become NULL values in your database. If you're analyzing this data, you need to handle these NULLs appropriately. For example, if you're looking at survey responses, you might want to count how many questions were left unanswered using COUNT(*) - COUNT(response).

Data quality often involves dealing with NULL values strategically. Sometimes, NULLs represent actual missing data that you need to collect. Other times, they might indicate optional information that isn't relevant for certain records. Understanding the difference helps you write better queries and maintain cleaner data.

The treatment of NULL values varies across different database systems, but the core concept remains the same: NULL represents unknown or missing information. This is different from zero, empty string, or false - those are known values. NULL means we don't know the value at all.

When grouping data, NULL values are typically grouped together. If you GROUP BY status, all records with NULL status will form their own group. This can be useful for identifying records that need attention or completion. However, you might sometimes want to treat NULLs differently, perhaps grouping them with a specific category using COALESCE.

Aggregate functions handle NULL values in specific ways. COUNT(*) counts all rows including those with NULL values, while COUNT(column_name) excludes NULL values. SUM, AVG, and other aggregate functions simply ignore NULL values in their calculations. Understanding these behaviors helps you write more accurate queries.

NULL values can also impact indexing and performance. Some database systems allow you to create indexes that exclude NULL values, which can improve query performance in certain scenarios. This is particularly useful when you know that NULL values aren't relevant to your common queries.

When designing databases, it's important to decide whether columns should allow NULL values. Making a column NOT NULL forces every record to have a value for that field. This might be appropriate for essential information like customer IDs or order dates, but could be too restrictive for optional information like middle names or secondary phone numbers.

Remember that NULL handling isn't just about writing correct queries - it's about understanding your data and making informed decisions about how to handle missing information. Should missing prices be treated as zeros? Should missing dates be replaced with a default value? These decisions depend entirely on your specific situation and business rules.

As you work with databases, you'll find that handling NULL values effectively is a key skill. Whether you're cleaning data, analyzing patterns, or generating reports, understanding how to work with missing information will help you write more robust and accurate queries.

14. Basic JOIN: Matching Your Shopping Lists

Let's explore how combining data from different tables is just like matching items between shopping lists. Imagine you have two shopping lists - one for the grocery store and one for the hardware store. Sometimes you need to compare these lists or combine them to plan your errands efficiently. This is exactly what JOIN operations do in SQL.

When you JOIN tables, you're connecting related information based on a common element. Think about how you might have a list of recipes and a separate list of ingredients. Each recipe refers to specific ingredients, and you want to see them together. The JOIN operation matches these related pieces of information, just like you might match a recipe card with the ingredients you need to buy.

The most common type of JOIN is called an INNER JOIN, though people often just write JOIN. It works like finding the overlap between two lists. Imagine you have a list of friends' birthdays and another list of addresses. When you JOIN these lists using someone's name as the connection point, you get a combined list showing both birthday and address information for each person who appears in both lists.

Let's look at a practical example. Suppose you have a table of orders and a table of customers. Each order has a customer ID that tells you who placed it. When you JOIN these tables, you're essentially saying "show me all orders along with the customer information for who placed them." The SQL would look something like: SELECT * FROM orders JOIN customers ON orders.customer_id = customers.id.

The ON clause in a JOIN is crucial - it's where you specify how the tables should be matched up. It's like saying "match these shopping lists wherever the store name is the same" or "connect these recipe cards with ingredients when the ingredient names match." You can think of it as drawing lines between related items on two different pages.

One common mistake when learning JOINs is forgetting to specify how the tables should be connected. If you forget the ON clause, you'll get what's called a Cartesian product - every row in the first table combined with every row in the second table. It's like taking your grocery list and matching each item with every item from your hardware store list, even when they're not related. This usually isn't what you want and can create huge result sets.

JOINs become particularly useful when you're working with data that's spread across multiple tables. Consider an online store where you have separate tables for products, orders, and customers. To see what products a specific customer has ordered, you need to JOIN all three tables together. The product information comes from one table, the order details from another, and the customer information from a third.

The order of tables in your JOIN matters for readability but not for performance. The database will figure out the most efficient way to combine the data. However, it's good practice to write your JOINs in a logical order that makes sense for someone reading your query. Start with the main table you're interested in, then JOIN to related tables in a way that tells a story.

Column names can sometimes be ambiguous when you're joining tables. If both tables have a column called "name," you need to specify which one you mean by using the table name or an alias. It's like saying "the name from the customer list" versus "the name from the order list." You can write customers.name or orders.name to be clear about which column you mean.

When working with JOINs, it's important to understand your data relationships. Some orders might have multiple items, meaning you'll get multiple rows in your results for a single order. This is normal and expected - it's like how a single shopping trip might include multiple items from your list. Understanding these one to many relationships helps you write better queries and understand your results.

Performance considerations become important as your tables grow larger. JOINing large tables can be resource intensive, so it's important to only JOIN the tables you need and only select the columns you're actually going to use. It's like making sure you only bring the shopping lists you need for today's errands, rather than carrying around every list you've ever made.

Joining tables is a fundamental operation in SQL that you'll use constantly. Whether you're analyzing sales data, generating reports, or just trying to get a complete picture of your data, JOINs are the tool that lets you bring related information together. The key is to think about how your data is connected and what relationships you're trying to show.

Remember that JOINs are just about matching related information. Don't let the technical terminology intimidate you. If you can understand how to match items between two shopping lists, you can understand how to JOIN tables in SQL. Start with simple JOINs between two tables, then gradually work your way up to more complex queries involving multiple tables as you become more comfortable with the concept.

15. Different Types of JOINs: Recipe Ingredients and Instructions

Building on our shopping list analogy, let's explore the different types of JOINs by thinking about recipes, ingredients, and cooking instructions. Imagine you're planning to cook dinner using several recipe cards and ingredient lists. Sometimes you need all the matching information, sometimes you want everything from one list regardless of matches, and sometimes you need to see what's missing.

The most common type of JOIN we covered previously was the INNER JOIN, which only shows matches between tables. But there are other types of JOINs that serve different purposes, just like how you might want to look at your recipe collection in different ways.

Let's start with LEFT JOIN (or LEFT OUTER JOIN - they're the same thing). A LEFT JOIN is like laying out all your recipe cards on the left side of the table and then trying to find matching ingredients from your pantry list on the right. You'll keep all the recipes, even if you don't have any of the ingredients. In SQL terms, this means you'll get all records from the left table (recipes) and any matching records from the right table (ingredients). If there's no match, you'll still see the recipe, but the ingredient fields will show as NULL.

Consider a practical example: you have a table of recipes and a table of reviews. Not every recipe has been reviewed yet, but you want to see all recipes along with any reviews they might have. Using a LEFT JOIN would show you every recipe, even those without reviews. It's like keeping track of all your recipes while noting which ones have feedback.

A RIGHT JOIN works the same way but in reverse - it keeps everything from the right table and matches what it can from the left. In practice, RIGHT JOINs are less common because you can usually rewrite them as LEFT JOINs by switching the table order. It's like flipping your recipe box around to look at it from a different angle.

FULL OUTER JOIN is like spreading out both your recipe cards and ingredient lists and keeping everything, regardless of matches. You'll see all recipes (even those without ingredients) and all ingredients (even those not used in any recipes). This is particularly useful when you're trying to find gaps in your data or ensure you haven't missed anything.

Consider a scenario where you're managing a restaurant's menu and inventory. A FULL OUTER JOIN between your menu items and available ingredients would show you both dishes you can't make because of missing ingredients and ingredients that aren't being used in any dishes. This helps with menu planning and inventory management.

One particularly interesting type of JOIN is the CROSS JOIN, which creates every possible combination between two tables. While less common, it's useful in specific scenarios. Imagine you offer a build your own sandwich menu with different breads and fillings. A CROSS JOIN would show every possible sandwich combination. It's like laying out all your bread options in rows and all your filling options in columns to see every possible pairing.

SELF JOINs, where you join a table to itself, are useful when dealing with hierarchical data. Think about a recipe that can be used as an ingredient in another recipe, like using homemade marinara sauce in your lasagna. You'd use a SELF JOIN to connect recipes to their component recipes.

The key to mastering different types of JOINs is understanding what data you want to keep and what you're willing to exclude. INNER JOINs are exclusive - they only show matches. LEFT and RIGHT JOINs keep everything from one side while matching what they can from the other. FULL OUTER JOINs keep everything from both sides. It's like deciding whether you want to see only recipes you can make with your current ingredients, all recipes regardless of ingredients, or everything including unused ingredients.

When working with multiple JOINs, the order of operations becomes important. Each JOIN creates an intermediate result that's then used for the next JOIN. It's like following a complex recipe where each step builds on the previous ones. The database optimizer will usually figure out the most efficient way to execute the JOINs, but understanding the logical flow helps you write better queries.

Error handling becomes particularly important with different types of JOINs. NULL values can propagate through your joins in unexpected ways, like a missing ingredient affecting multiple recipes. It's important to use COALESCE or ISNULL functions to handle these cases gracefully, providing default values where appropriate.

Performance considerations vary between JOIN types. INNER JOINs can be more efficient because they only process matching records, while OUTER JOINs need to process and preserve unmatched records. It's like how checking only the recipes you can make with your current ingredients is faster than going through your entire recipe collection.

The choice of JOIN type should be driven by your business requirements rather than performance concerns. If you need to see all customers, including those who haven't placed orders, use a LEFT JOIN even if an INNER JOIN might be faster. Clarity and correctness should be your primary concerns.

Remember that JOINs are just tools for combining related data in different ways. The type of JOIN you choose depends on what information you need to see and what you're willing to exclude. Start by clearly identifying what data you need to keep, then choose the appropriate JOIN type to achieve that result. With practice, selecting the right type of JOIN becomes as natural as deciding how to organize your recipe collection.

16. Multiple JOINs: Planning a Wedding Seating Chart

Planning a wedding seating chart is the perfect analogy for understanding how to work with multiple JOINs in SQL. Just as you need to consider various lists and relationships when arranging wedding tables, complex database queries often require combining multiple tables in specific ways to get the information you need.

Imagine you're planning a wedding for 200 guests. You have several lists to work with: the main guest list, dietary restrictions, family relationships, plus ones, and table assignments. Each of these lists contains different but related information that needs to come together to create the perfect seating arrangement. This is exactly like working with multiple JOINs in SQL.

Let's start with a practical example. You might have a guests table containing basic information about each attendee, a dietary_restrictions table listing specific food requirements, and a relationships table showing how guests are connected to each other. To create a comprehensive seating chart, you need to combine all this information in a meaningful way.

The first step might be joining the guests table with the dietary_restrictions table to ensure nobody with a seafood allergy ends up at a table being served shellfish. This is like our basic JOIN operations, but we're not stopping there. We then need to join this result with the relationships table to make sure we're seating family members appropriately – perhaps keeping certain relatives together while separating others who don't get along.

In SQL, this might look like joining three or more tables together. Each JOIN creates an intermediate result that becomes the foundation for the next JOIN, just like how you might first group guests by family, then consider dietary restrictions, and finally factor in personal preferences.

One common challenge when working with multiple JOINs is maintaining data clarity. Just as you wouldn't want to lose track of any guests while planning the seating chart, you need to be careful not to accidentally exclude data when joining multiple tables. This is where choosing the right type of JOIN for each connection becomes crucial.

Think about the plus ones situation. Some guests are bringing partners while others aren't. If you used only INNER JOINs, you might accidentally exclude single guests from your seating plan. Instead, you'd want to use a LEFT JOIN to keep all guests in your list, whether or not they have a plus one. Then you might use another LEFT JOIN to add dietary information, again ensuring no guests are accidentally dropped from the list.

Performance becomes increasingly important as you add more JOINs to your query. Just as you wouldn't want to review your entire guest list every time you make a single table assignment, databases need efficient ways to handle multiple JOINs. This is where proper indexing and query optimization come into play.

Sometimes you'll need to use subqueries or common table expressions (CTEs) to break down complex multiple JOIN operations into more manageable pieces. It's like creating smaller groups of guests based on certain criteria before making the final seating arrangements. This can make your queries easier to understand and maintain.

Error handling becomes particularly important with multiple JOINs. You need to account for missing data, just as you need a plan for last-minute wedding cancellations or unexpected plus ones. Using appropriate NULL handling and data validation becomes crucial when working with multiple joined tables.

The order of JOINs can affect both the performance and results of your query. While the database optimizer will usually figure out the most efficient execution plan, understanding how JOIN order impacts your results helps you write better queries. It's like knowing that you should probably figure out family groupings before assigning specific seats.

Always consider what data you actually need. Just as you wouldn't track shoe sizes for a wedding seating chart, avoid joining to tables that don't contribute necessary information to your final result. Each additional JOIN adds complexity and potential performance overhead to your query.

Testing becomes increasingly important as you add more JOINs. Start with a small subset of data and verify that your joins are working as expected before applying them to the full dataset. This is like doing a test run of your seating arrangements with just the wedding party before tackling the entire guest list.

Remember that multiple JOINs are often necessary to answer real-world questions, but they should be used judiciously. Each JOIN should serve a specific purpose in your final result set. Keep your queries focused on the data you need, just as you keep your seating chart focused on creating comfortable and practical arrangements for your guests.

The key to success with multiple JOINs is maintaining a clear understanding of how each table relates to the others and what information you need in your final result. Start with the most important relationships and build from there, testing at each step to ensure you're maintaining data integrity and query performance.

17. Aliases: Giving Nicknames to Friends

Just as we give nicknames to our friends to make conversations easier and more personal, SQL aliases serve a similar purpose in database queries. They provide shorter, more convenient names for tables and columns, making our queries both more readable and easier to write.

Think about how you might refer to your friend Elizabeth as "Liz" or Christopher as "Chris." These nicknames make casual conversation flow more naturally while still clearly identifying who you're talking about. SQL aliases work the same way, letting us assign temporary, friendly names to database objects while we're working with them.

Let's start with a common scenario where aliases become invaluable. Imagine you're working with a customer order database that has a long table name like customer_purchase_history. Writing this full name repeatedly in a query becomes tedious and makes the code harder to read. By giving this table an alias like "orders," we can write clearer, more concise queries while still working with all the same data.

Column aliases are particularly useful when working with calculated fields or when you want to make your output more user friendly. Instead of seeing a column header like annual_revenue_usd, you might prefer to display it as "Annual Revenue" in your reports. Aliases let you make these kinds of presentational changes without altering the underlying database structure.

There are two main ways to create aliases in SQL. The first uses the AS keyword explicitly, while the second simply places the alias after the table or column name with a space between them. Both approaches are valid, though using AS makes your intentions clearer and can help prevent confusion, especially for those new to SQL.

When working with multiple tables, aliases become essential for avoiding ambiguity. Consider a query that joins an employees table with a departments table, both of which might have a "name" column. Without aliases, you'd need to write the full table name each time you reference a column: employees.name or departments.name. With aliases, you could simply write e.name or d.name, making your query much more manageable.

One common convention when choosing aliases is to use the first letter or a meaningful abbreviation of the table name. For example, customers might become c, products might become p, and orders might become o. While this works well for simple queries, be careful not to make your aliases too cryptic in complex queries involving many tables. The goal is to improve readability, not create a puzzle.

Something to keep in mind is that aliases exist only for the duration of the query. They don't change anything in the database itself, and you'll need to declare them again in each new query where you want to use them. This is similar to how a nickname might be used among certain friends but isn't a legal name change.

Aliases are particularly powerful when working with self joins, where you need to reference the same table multiple times in a query. Imagine tracking employee relationships where each employee has a manager who is also an employee. You might alias the employees table as "workers" and "managers" to clearly distinguish the two roles you're querying.

When using aliases with JOINs, you can reference the alias immediately after declaring it in the same query. This means you can use the shorter name throughout your JOIN conditions and WHERE clauses, making complex queries much easier to write and understand. It's like introducing someone by their full name once, then using their nickname for the rest of the conversation.

A practical tip when using aliases is to choose names that make sense in the context of your query. While single-letter aliases might be fine for simple queries, more descriptive aliases can make complex queries self-documenting. For example, instead of "c" for customers, you might use "active_customers" or "new_customers" if that better describes the subset of data you're working with.

Error handling becomes important when working with aliases, particularly in complex queries. If you reference an alias before it's declared or try to use an alias from an outer query in a subquery where it's not visible, your query will fail. Understanding the scope of aliases helps prevent these kinds of errors.

Column aliases are especially useful when working with aggregate functions or calculations. Instead of seeing sum(purchase_amount) in your results, you might prefer "Total Sales." These friendly names make your query results more accessible to non-technical users who need to understand the data.

Remember that while aliases can make your queries more readable and maintainable, they should be used thoughtfully. Like any nickname, an alias should make communication clearer, not more confusing. Choose aliases that are meaningful in the context of your query and consistent with any naming conventions your team uses.

Finally, consider documenting any non-obvious aliases in your query comments, especially for complex queries that others might need to maintain. Just as you might need to explain to a new friend that "Buzz" is actually William's nickname, a brief comment can help future readers understand your alias choices and the logic behind your query structure.

18. GROUP BY: Summarizing Your Monthly Expenses

Managing personal finances is a lot like organizing receipts at the end of the month, and GROUP BY in SQL helps us do exactly that kind of summarization. Just as you might sort your monthly expenses into categories like groceries, utilities, and entertainment, GROUP BY allows us to create meaningful summaries of our data.

Let's imagine you're tracking your daily expenses in a database. Each purchase you make is a single row recording the date, amount, category, and payment method. While having this detailed information is useful, sometimes you want to step back and see the bigger picture, like how much you spent in total on groceries last month or which payment method you use most frequently.

This is where GROUP BY shines. Instead of looking at individual transactions, it allows us to cluster our data into meaningful groups and then calculate summaries for each group. Think of it like sorting your physical receipts into different piles based on their categories, then adding up each pile to see your total spending in each area.

One of the most common use cases for GROUP BY is analyzing spending patterns. For example, you might want to know your total spending by category for each month. Without GROUP BY, you'd need to manually filter and add up all the grocery purchases, then all the utility payments, and so on. With GROUP BY, a single query can give you these totals automatically.

The real power of GROUP BY becomes apparent when we combine it with aggregate functions like SUM, COUNT, AVG, MAX, and MIN. These functions perform calculations on each group of data rather than on individual rows. It's like being able to instantly know not just your total grocery spending, but also your average grocery bill, your largest single purchase, and how many times you went to the grocery store.

When working with GROUP BY, it's important to understand that any column in your SELECT statement must either be included in the GROUP BY clause or be used within an aggregate function. This makes sense when you think about it: if you're grouping expenses by category, each group needs to have a single value to display. You can't show individual transaction dates within a grouped summary unless you're using them to calculate something like the most recent purchase date.

Let's consider a practical example. Imagine tracking your household utility bills over time. Each bill record includes the utility type (electricity, water, gas), the amount, and the billing date. By using GROUP BY with your utility records, you could easily see your average monthly cost for each utility type, identify which utility has the highest total cost, or track how many bills you receive for each service annually.

The order of operations in a query with GROUP BY is important to understand. First, the database processes any WHERE conditions to filter the rows. Then it groups the remaining rows according to your GROUP BY clause. Finally, it applies any aggregate functions to each group. Understanding this sequence helps you write more effective queries and troubleshoot when results don't match your expectations.

You can group by multiple columns too, creating more specific categorizations. For instance, you might group your expenses by both category and payment method to see patterns like how much you typically charge to your credit card for groceries versus how much you pay in cash. Each unique combination of the grouped columns becomes its own group in the results.

A common gotcha when working with GROUP BY is forgetting that it creates a summary view of your data. Once you've grouped your results, you can't reference individual row details unless they're part of the grouping or an aggregate calculation. This is similar to how, once you've sorted your physical receipts into piles by category, you can't talk about individual receipts without digging back into the specific pile.

Time-based grouping is particularly useful for financial analysis. You might group transactions by month, quarter, or year to identify spending trends over time. SQL provides various date functions that can help extract these time periods from your transaction dates, making it easy to create meaningful time-based summaries.

When working with grouped data, it's often helpful to include count calculations alongside your other aggregates. This gives context to your summaries by showing how many records went into each group. For example, knowing you spent $500 on restaurants in a month becomes more meaningful when you also know this represents 10 separate meals.

GROUP BY becomes even more powerful when combined with JOINs. You might join your expenses table with a categories table that contains category descriptions and budget limits, then group by category to compare actual spending against budgeted amounts. This kind of analysis can quickly highlight areas where spending might be exceeding planned limits.

Remember that GROUP BY performs its grouping on the values exactly as they appear in the database. If you need to group similar but not identical values (like grouping "Groceries" with "GROCERIES"), you'll need to standardize these values either in your data or as part of your query using string functions.

As your queries become more complex, maintaining readability becomes crucial. Using aliases and meaningful column names for your aggregated values helps make the results more understandable. Instead of sum(amount), you might use sum(amount) as total_spent or avg(amount) as average_purchase.

Through thoughtful use of GROUP BY, you can transform detailed transaction records into meaningful financial summaries that help you understand spending patterns, track budgets, and make informed decisions about your finances. Just as you might periodically review your sorted receipts to understand your spending habits, GROUP BY helps you regularly analyze and monitor your financial data in a systematic way.

19. Aggregate Functions: Analyzing Your Fitness Tracker Data

Imagine your fitness tracker diligently recording every step, heartbeat, and workout throughout your day. While having this detailed data is great, the real insights come from summarizing it in meaningful ways. This is where SQL's aggregate functions come in – they're like your fitness app's dashboard, taking all those individual measurements and turning them into useful summaries that help you track your progress.

Understanding Aggregate Functions

Just as your fitness tracker doesn't just show you every single heartbeat but instead gives you averages, maximums, and totals, SQL's aggregate functions process multiple rows of data to produce single summary values. The five most common aggregate functions are:

COUNT(): Counts the number of rows or values

SUM(): Adds up numeric values

AVG(): Calculates the average of numeric values

MAX(): Finds the highest value

MIN(): Finds the lowest value

Let's look at each of these functions using a fitness tracking database. Imagine you have a table called daily_activities that records your exercise data:

```
SELECT COUNT(*) as total_workouts
FROM daily_activities;
```

This query tells you how many workouts you've logged, just like checking your streak on your fitness app.

To find your total steps for the month:

```
SELECT SUM(steps) as monthly_steps
FROM daily_activities
```

WHERE MONTH(activity_date) = MONTH(CURRENT_DATE);

Want to know your average daily heart rate?

SELECT AVG(avg_heart_rate) as typical_heart_rate

FROM daily_activities;

To see your longest workout:

SELECT MAX(duration_minutes) as longest_session

FROM daily_activities;

Or find your fastest mile time:

SELECT MIN(mile_time_minutes) as best_mile

FROM daily_activities

WHERE activity_type = 'Running';

Combining Aggregate Functions

The real power comes from using multiple aggregate functions together. For example, to get a complete workout summary:

SELECT

COUNT(*) as total_workouts,

AVG(duration_minutes) as avg_workout_length,

MAX(steps) as most_steps,

MIN(steps) as least_steps,

SUM(calories_burned) as total_calories

FROM daily_activities;

Working with Nulls

Sometimes your fitness tracker might miss recording certain metrics. Aggregate functions handle NULL values differently:

- COUNT(*) counts all rows

- COUNT(column_name) counts only non-NULL values

- Other aggregate functions (SUM, AVG, MAX, MIN) ignore NULL values

For example, if some heart rate readings are missing:

SELECT

COUNT(*) as total_readings,

```
COUNT(heart_rate) as valid_heart_readings,
AVG(heart_rate) as average_heart_rate
FROM heart_rate_logs;
```

Using DISTINCT with Aggregates

To count unique values, combine DISTINCT with aggregate functions. For instance, to see how many different types of exercises you've done:

```
SELECT COUNT(DISTINCT activity_type) as exercise_variety
FROM daily_activities;
```

Grouping with Aggregates

Aggregate functions become even more powerful when combined with GROUP BY. To see your average steps for each day of the week:

```
SELECT
DAYNAME(activity_date) as day_of_week,
AVG(steps) as average_steps
FROM daily_activities
GROUP BY DAYNAME(activity_date);
```

Common Use Cases

1. Progress Tracking:
- Total monthly distance covered
- Weekly step count averages
- Personal records for different exercises

2. Health Monitoring:
- Daily average heart rate trends
- Maximum heart rate during workouts
- Total active minutes per week

3. Workout Analysis:
- Most common workout types
- Average duration by exercise type
- Calorie burn patterns

4. Goal Setting:

- Distance covered versus targets
- Workout frequency analysis
- Progress towards yearly goals

Best Practices

1. Always consider what NULL values mean in your data and handle them appropriately
2. Use meaningful aliases for aggregate calculations to make your results clear
3. Remember that aggregate functions can only be used in:
- SELECT clause
- HAVING clause
- ORDER BY clause
4. Consider data accuracy when using aggregates:
- Are there outliers skewing your averages?
- Should you filter out certain data points?
- Would median values be more meaningful than averages?

Troubleshooting Tips

If your aggregate results seem incorrect, check:

- NULL handling in your data
- WHERE clause filtering
- Date range accuracy
- Unit consistency (e.g., mixing miles and kilometers)

Common Mistakes to Avoid

1. Mixing aggregate and non-aggregate columns without GROUP BY
2. Forgetting to filter data before aggregating
3. Using COUNT(*) when COUNT(column_name) would be more appropriate
4. Not considering data quality issues

Practice Exercises

1. Calculate your average daily steps for each month of the year
2. Find your three longest workouts ever recorded

3. Compare your workout frequency between weekdays and weekends

4. Calculate your total distance covered by activity type

Summary

Aggregate functions are essential tools for analyzing fitness data, turning thousands of individual measurements into meaningful insights. By combining these functions with other SQL features like GROUP BY and WHERE clauses, you can create powerful analyses of your fitness progress and patterns. Just as your fitness tracker's app shows you daily, weekly, and monthly summaries, SQL's aggregate functions help you understand your fitness data at whatever level of detail you need.

Remember: The goal of using aggregate functions is to transform raw data into actionable insights that can help you track progress, set goals, and maintain motivation in your fitness journey. Whether you're tracking steps, monitoring heart rate, or analyzing workout patterns, aggregate functions help you see the bigger picture of your fitness progress.

20. HAVING: Filtering Group Results Like Budget Categories

Imagine you've organized all your monthly expenses into neat categories using GROUP BY, but now you want to focus on just the categories where you're overspending. This is where the HAVING clause comes in – it's like a second filter that works on your grouped results, helping you identify categories that meet specific criteria based on their summary values.

The HAVING Difference

Think of WHERE and HAVING as two different types of filters:

- WHERE filters individual rows before they're grouped (like excluding all cash transactions)

- HAVING filters groups after they're created (like showing only categories where total spending exceeds $500)

For example, to see only expense categories where you've spent more than $500 in total:

```
SELECT
category,
SUM(amount) as total_spent
FROM expenses
GROUP BY category
HAVING SUM(amount) > 500;
```

The Budget Monitor

Let's say you have monthly budget limits for different categories. To find categories where you're exceeding the budget:

```
SELECT
category,
SUM(amount) as total_spent,
MAX(budget_limit) as monthly_budget
FROM expenses
```

JOIN budget_categories ON expenses.category = budget_categories.category
GROUP BY category
HAVING SUM(amount) > MAX(budget_limit);

Common HAVING Use Cases

1. High-Spending Categories:

Find categories where spending is above average:

```
SELECT
category,
SUM(amount) as total_spent
FROM expenses
GROUP BY category
HAVING total_spent > (
SELECT AVG(total)
FROM (
SELECT SUM(amount) as total
FROM expenses
GROUP BY category
) category_totals
);
```

2. Frequent Transactions:

Identify categories with unusually high transaction counts:

```
SELECT
category,
COUNT(*) as transaction_count
FROM expenses
GROUP BY category
HAVING transaction_count > 10;
```

3. Budget Variance Analysis:

Find categories with the highest budget overruns:

```
SELECT
category,
```

```
SUM(amount) as actual_spent,
MAX(budget_limit) as budget,
(SUM(amount) - MAX(budget_limit)) as variance
FROM expenses
JOIN budget_categories USING (category)
GROUP BY category
HAVING variance > 0
ORDER BY variance DESC;
```

Multiple Conditions

You can combine multiple conditions in HAVING, just like with WHERE:

```
SELECT
category,
COUNT(*) as transactions,
SUM(amount) as total_spent
FROM expenses
GROUP BY category
HAVING transactions >= 5
AND total_spent > 1000;
```

HAVING vs WHERE: When to Use Each

Use WHERE when:

- Filtering individual transactions (amount > 100)
- Checking non-aggregated values (date > '2024-01-01')
- Filtering before grouping for better performance

Use HAVING when:

- Filtering based on aggregate values (SUM, COUNT, AVG)
- Working with grouped results
- Needing to reference aggregate calculations

Common Patterns

1. Finding Significant Groups:

Show only categories that represent significant spending:

```
SELECT
```

```
category,
SUM(amount) as total,
COUNT(*) as transactions
FROM expenses
GROUP BY category
HAVING total > 1000 AND transactions >= 3;
```

2. Comparing to Averages:

Categories spending more than 50% above average:

```
SELECT
category,
AVG(amount) as avg_transaction
FROM expenses
GROUP BY category
HAVING avg_transaction > (
SELECT AVG(amount) * 1.5
FROM expenses
);
```

3. Trend Analysis:

Categories with increasing monthly totals:

```
SELECT
category,
MAX(monthly_total) - MIN(monthly_total) as trend
FROM (
SELECT
category,
DATE_FORMAT(date, '%Y-%m') as month,
SUM(amount) as monthly_total
FROM expenses
GROUP BY category, month
) monthly_totals
GROUP BY category
HAVING trend > 0;
```

Best Practices

1. Use clear naming for aggregated values
2. Consider performance implications of complex HAVING conditions
3. Double-check your logic when combining WHERE and HAVING
4. Use comments to explain complex filtering logic

Common Mistakes

1. Trying to use HAVING without GROUP BY
2. Confusing WHERE and HAVING roles
3. Referencing non-aggregated columns in HAVING
4. Forgetting that HAVING works on groups, not individual rows

Practice Exercises

1. Find categories where the average transaction is over $100
2. Identify months where total spending exceeded the previous month
3. List categories with more than 5 transactions but less than $1000 total
4. Show categories where the maximum transaction is more than twice the average

Summary

HAVING is your tool for filtering grouped results based on aggregate values. While WHERE helps you filter individual records, HAVING lets you focus on the groups that matter most. Whether you're tracking budget categories that need attention, identifying spending patterns, or monitoring transaction frequencies, HAVING helps you zero in on the most relevant summary data.

Remember: Combined with GROUP BY and aggregate functions, HAVING gives you powerful control over your grouped data analysis. It's the final piece that lets you focus on just the summary results that matter most for your budget analysis and financial decision-making.

21. Subqueries: Making Complex Decisions

Subqueries are like making complex decisions that require multiple steps of thinking - similar to planning a vacation where you first need to figure out which destinations are within your budget before you can choose the one with the best weather. In our daily lives, we often make decisions that depend on other decisions, and subqueries work the same way in SQL.

Let's start with a simple example that everyone can relate to. Imagine you're trying to find out which of your monthly expenses are above your average spending. You can't just look at the amounts directly - first you need to calculate the average, and then compare each expense to that average. In SQL, this becomes a subquery where one query (finding the average) needs to run before the main query can compare expenses to that average.

Consider a table called monthly_expenses with columns for expense_id, category, and amount. To find expenses above average, we would write:

```
SELECT category, amount
FROM monthly_expenses
WHERE amount > (SELECT AVG(amount) FROM monthly_expenses);
```

The part in parentheses is our subquery - it runs first to calculate the average, and then the main query uses that result to filter the expenses. This is like first calculating your monthly budget before deciding which purchases are too expensive.

Subqueries can appear in different parts of your main query. They can be in the WHERE clause (as we just saw), in the SELECT list, or even in the FROM clause. Think of it like preparing a meal - sometimes you need to prepare ingredients before cooking (WHERE), sometimes you need to calculate portions while serving (SELECT), and sometimes you need to combine prepared dishes before final assembly (FROM).

Let's look at a more complex real-world scenario. Suppose you're managing an online store and want to find customers who have spent more than the average customer in each state. This requires nested thinking: first, you need to calculate the average spending per state, then compare each customer's spending to their state's average. Here's how that might look:

```
SELECT customer_name, state, total_spending
FROM customer_sales
WHERE total_spending > (
SELECT AVG(total_spending)
FROM customer_sales AS state_avg
WHERE state_avg.state = customer_sales.state
);
```

This is called a correlated subquery because the inner query references the outer query's table. It's like checking each customer's spending against their own state's average, rather than the national average.

Subqueries can also be used to create derived tables in the FROM clause. Imagine you're analyzing sales data and want to compare each department's performance to the previous year, but first you need to calculate yearly totals. You might write:

```
SELECT dept_name,
current_year_sales,
previous_year_sales,
((current_year_sales - previous_year_sales) / previous_year_sales *
100) as growth_percentage
FROM (
SELECT department.name as dept_name,
SUM(CASE WHEN YEAR(sale_date) = 2023 THEN amount
ELSE 0 END) as current_year_sales,
```

```
SUM(CASE WHEN YEAR(sale_date) = 2022 THEN amount ELSE 0 END) as previous_year_sales
FROM sales
JOIN department ON sales.dept_id = department.id
GROUP BY department.name
) yearly_comparison;
```

This query first creates a derived table with yearly totals, then calculates the growth percentage in the main query. It's like preparing a summary report before analyzing the trends.

One common use of subqueries is in the IN clause, where you want to filter based on a list of values that needs to be calculated. For example, finding all products that have been ordered in the last month:

```
SELECT product_name, price
FROM products
WHERE product_id IN (
SELECT DISTINCT product_id
FROM orders
WHERE order_date >= DATEADD(month, -1, GETDATE())
);
```

Sometimes you need to use EXISTS or NOT EXISTS with subqueries to check whether certain conditions are true. This is like checking off items on a to-do list. For example, finding customers who haven't placed any orders this year:

```
SELECT customer_name, email
FROM customers c
WHERE NOT EXISTS (
SELECT 1
FROM orders o
WHERE o.customer_id = c.customer_id
AND YEAR(order_date) = 2023
);
```

A powerful feature of subqueries is that they can be used to create calculated columns in your SELECT list. Imagine you want to show each product's price along with how it compares to the average price in its category:

```
SELECT product_name,
price,
(SELECT AVG(price) FROM products p2 WHERE p2.category = p1.category) as category_average,
price - (SELECT AVG(price) FROM products p2 WHERE p2.category = p1.category) as price_difference
FROM products p1;
```

Remember that while subqueries are powerful, they can also impact performance if not used carefully. It's like taking a longer route to your destination - sometimes it's necessary, but you should always consider whether there's a more direct path. In many cases, JOINs can be used instead of subqueries and might perform better.

When writing subqueries, it's important to keep them focused and readable. Break down complex problems into smaller steps, and consider whether a Common Table Expression (which we'll cover in the next chapter) might make your query easier to understand.

Practice writing subqueries by starting with simple examples and gradually building up to more complex ones. Try to identify situations in your daily work where you need to make decisions based on other calculations or conditions - these are often perfect candidates for subqueries. Remember that like any tool in SQL, subqueries are meant to help you solve real-world problems more effectively, not to make your queries unnecessarily complicated.

22. Common Table Expressions: Breaking Down Big Problems

Common Table Expressions, often called CTEs, are like breaking down a complex recipe into manageable steps. Instead of trying to cook everything at once, you write down each step separately, making the whole process easier to understand and follow. They provide a way to organize and simplify complicated queries by splitting them into logical pieces, similar to how you might tackle a big home improvement project by dividing it into smaller tasks.

Let's start with a simple example that everyone can understand. Imagine you're tracking your daily steps and want to find out which days you exceeded your average step count. Instead of nesting queries inside each other, you can write it clearly using a CTE:

```
WITH daily_average AS (
SELECT AVG(step_count) as avg_steps
FROM daily_activity
)
SELECT activity_date, step_count
FROM daily_activity, daily_average
WHERE step_count > avg_steps
ORDER BY activity_date;
```

This is much easier to read than a nested subquery because it breaks the problem into two clear steps: first calculate the average, then find the days above that average. It's like writing down your shopping list before going to the store, instead of trying to remember everything while walking through the aisles.

CTEs become even more valuable when you need to reference the same intermediate result multiple times. Consider analyzing your monthly budget where you want to compare expenses across different categories to their respective averages. Without a CTE, you'd need to calculate category averages repeatedly. With a CTE, you calculate it once and use it multiple times:

```
WITH category_averages AS (
SELECT category,
AVG(amount) as avg_amount,
COUNT(*) as transaction_count
FROM expenses
GROUP BY category
)
SELECT e.category,
e.amount,
ca.avg_amount,
e.amount - ca.avg_amount as difference_from_average,
ca.transaction_count
FROM expenses e
JOIN category_averages ca ON e.category = ca.category
WHERE e.amount > ca.avg_amount * 1.5;
```

One of the most powerful features of CTEs is that they can be chained together, each building upon the results of previous ones. This is particularly useful when you need to perform multiple transformations on your data, like analyzing sales trends over different time periods:

```
WITH monthly_sales AS (
SELECT
DATE_TRUNC('month', sale_date) as month,
SUM(amount) as total_sales
FROM sales
GROUP BY DATE_TRUNC('month', sale_date)
),
rolling_average AS (
SELECT month,
total_sales,
```

```
AVG(total_sales) OVER (
ORDER BY month
ROWS BETWEEN 2 PRECEDING AND CURRENT ROW
) as three_month_average
FROM monthly_sales
)
SELECT
month,
total_sales,
three_month_average,
total_sales - three_month_average as variance
FROM rolling_average
ORDER BY month;
```

CTEs can also be recursive, meaning they can reference themselves. This is particularly useful when dealing with hierarchical data, like organizational charts or family trees. Imagine you want to trace all the managers above an employee:

```
WITH RECURSIVE manager_chain AS (
SELECT employee_id, manager_id, name, 1 as level
FROM employees
WHERE employee_id = 100
UNION ALL
SELECT e.employee_id, e.manager_id, e.name, mc.level + 1
FROM employees e
JOIN manager_chain mc ON e.employee_id = mc.manager_id
)
SELECT name, level
FROM manager_chain
ORDER BY level;
```

When working with complex data transformations, CTEs can make your code much more maintainable. Instead of having one massive query, you can break it down into logical steps. For example, analyzing customer purchasing patterns might involve several stages:

```
WITH customer_purchases AS (
SELECT customer_id,
COUNT(*) as total_orders,
SUM(amount) as total_spent
FROM orders
GROUP BY customer_id
),
customer_segments AS (
SELECT *,
CASE
WHEN total_spent > 1000 THEN 'High Value'
WHEN total_spent > 500 THEN 'Medium Value'
ELSE 'Low Value'
END as segment
FROM customer_purchases
),
segment_analysis AS (
SELECT segment,
COUNT(*) as customer_count,
AVG(total_orders) as avg_orders,
AVG(total_spent) as avg_spent
FROM customer_segments
GROUP BY segment
)
SELECT *
FROM segment_analysis
ORDER BY avg_spent DESC;
```

CTEs also help with query optimization because they make it easier for the database engine to understand and optimize your query plan. They're like giving clear directions to someone instead of a confusing set of interconnected instructions.

Remember that while CTEs can make your queries more readable and maintainable, they don't necessarily improve performance compared to equivalent subqueries or joins. The database engine usually treats them similarly to subqueries when executing the query. The main benefits are in code organization and readability.

When writing CTEs, try to give them meaningful names that describe what they're calculating or preparing. This makes your queries self-documenting and easier for others to understand. Also, keep each CTE focused on a single logical task, just like you would when breaking down any complex project into manageable pieces.

Practice using CTEs by taking complex queries you've written with nested subqueries and rewriting them using CTEs. You'll often find that the resulting code is clearer and easier to maintain. Start with simple examples and gradually work your way up to more complex scenarios as you become comfortable with the syntax and concepts.

23. Views: Creating Shortcuts for Regular Reports

Views in SQL are like creating custom shortcuts or saved reports that you can easily access later. Think of them as pre-made templates that save you from writing the same complex queries over and over again. Just as you might create a shortcut on your computer desktop to quickly access frequently used files, views provide instant access to commonly needed data combinations.

Let's start with a simple example that demonstrates why views are useful. Imagine you run a small online bookstore and frequently need to check which books are running low on stock. Instead of writing the same inventory query every time, you can create a view:

```
CREATE VIEW low_stock_books AS
SELECT title, author, quantity_on_hand, reorder_point
FROM books
WHERE quantity_on_hand <= reorder_point;
```

Now whenever you need this information, you can simply query the view as if it were a regular table: SELECT * FROM low_stock_books. The view automatically runs the underlying query and returns fresh results each time.

Views serve multiple purposes beyond just convenience. They can help simplify complex queries, enhance security by restricting access to certain data, and ensure consistency across your organization. Consider a situation where your sales team needs regular access to customer purchase history, but you want to hide sensitive information like credit card details. You can create a view that shows only the appropriate data:

```
CREATE VIEW customer_purchase_summary AS
SELECT
c.customer_name,
o.order_date,
```

```
o.total_amount,
p.product_name,
p.category
FROM customers c
JOIN orders o ON c.customer_id = o.customer_id
JOIN order_items oi ON o.order_id = oi.order_id
JOIN products p ON oi.product_id = p.product_id;
```

Views can also incorporate calculations and data transformations. If you regularly analyze sales performance, you might create a view that automatically calculates various metrics:

```
CREATE VIEW sales_metrics AS
SELECT
DATE_TRUNC('month', sale_date) as month,
SUM(amount) as total_sales,
COUNT(DISTINCT customer_id) as unique_customers,
SUM(amount) / COUNT(DISTINCT customer_id) as
average_customer_spend,
SUM(quantity) as units_sold
FROM sales
GROUP BY DATE_TRUNC('month', sale_date);
```

One powerful feature of views is their ability to hide the complexity of joins and subqueries from end users. Instead of requiring everyone to understand complex database relationships, you can create intuitive views that present data in a user-friendly format. For example, a view for tracking inventory across multiple warehouses might look like this:

```
CREATE VIEW inventory_status AS
WITH stock_levels AS (
SELECT
product_id,
warehouse_id,
quantity_on_hand,
```

```
LAG(quantity_on_hand) OVER (
PARTITION BY product_id, warehouse_id
ORDER BY last_updated
) as previous_quantity
FROM inventory_history
WHERE last_updated >= CURRENT_DATE - INTERVAL '30
days'
)
SELECT
p.product_name,
w.warehouse_name,
s.quantity_on_hand,
s.quantity_on_hand - s.previous_quantity as monthly_change
FROM stock_levels s
JOIN products p ON s.product_id = p.product_id
JOIN warehouses w ON s.warehouse_id = w.warehouse_id;
```

Views can be particularly useful when working with data that needs to be formatted or presented in specific ways for different audiences. For instance, you might create separate views for financial reporting that handle currency conversions and formatting:

```
CREATE VIEW financial_summary AS
SELECT
transaction_date,
ROUND(amount_usd, 2) as amount_usd,
ROUND(amount_usd * exchange_rate, 2) as amount_local,
category,
CASE
WHEN amount_usd >= 1000000 THEN 'High Value'
WHEN amount_usd >= 100000 THEN 'Medium Value'
ELSE 'Low Value'
END as transaction_tier
FROM transactions
```

JOIN exchange_rates ON transactions.currency = exchange_rates.currency

WHERE transaction_date >= CURRENT_DATE - INTERVAL '1 year';

Some databases support materialized views, which actually store the result set and periodically refresh it. These are particularly useful for complex calculations that don't need real-time updates. Think of them like a cached version of your query results:

```
CREATE MATERIALIZED VIEW monthly_sales_summary AS
SELECT
product_category,
DATE_TRUNC('month', sale_date) as month,
COUNT(*) as total_sales,
SUM(amount) as revenue,
AVG(amount) as average_sale_value
FROM sales
GROUP BY product_category, DATE_TRUNC('month', sale_date)
WITH DATA;
```

Views can also be used to implement row-level security by incorporating user-specific filters. For example, you might create a view that only shows orders relevant to a specific sales representative:

```
CREATE VIEW my_customer_orders AS
SELECT
c.customer_name,
o.order_date,
o.total_amount,
o.status
FROM orders o
JOIN customers c ON o.customer_id = c.customer_id
WHERE o.sales_rep_id = CURRENT_USER_ID();
```

When creating views, it's important to consider performance implications. While views make queries easier to write and maintain, they don't automatically improve performance. In fact, complex views with multiple joins and subqueries might perform worse than direct table queries. Always test your views with realistic data volumes and consider creating indexes to support common query patterns.

Remember that views can be used as building blocks for other views, but be careful not to create too many layers of nested views as this can make troubleshooting difficult and impact performance. Keep your view definitions focused and documented, just as you would with any other code component.

Finally, views can be invaluable for managing database changes. If you need to modify the underlying table structure, you can often update the view definition while maintaining the same interface for your applications. This provides a layer of abstraction that can make database maintenance and upgrades much smoother.

24. INSERT Statements: Adding Items to Your Pantry

Adding new items to a database is like stocking your pantry - you need to be organized and precise about what goes where. The INSERT statement is your tool for adding new records, and understanding how to use it effectively is crucial for maintaining your data.

Let's start with the most basic form of adding a single item. Imagine you just bought a new jar of pasta sauce and want to add it to your pantry tracking system. The syntax is straightforward:

INSERT INTO pantry (item_name, quantity, expiration_date) VALUES ('Marinara Sauce', 1, '2024-12-31');

This command tells the database three things: which table to add to (pantry), what information you're providing (the columns), and the actual values. Just like you wouldn't put groceries away without knowing where they belong, you need to be specific about which columns will receive the new data.

Sometimes you'll want to add multiple items at once, perhaps after a big grocery shopping trip. SQL allows you to insert multiple rows in a single statement, which is more efficient than doing them one at a time:

INSERT INTO pantry (item_name, quantity, expiration_date) VALUES

('Spaghetti', 2, '2025-06-30'),

('Olive Oil', 1, '2024-08-15'),

('Black Pepper', 1, NULL);

Notice how we handled the black pepper - since it doesn't really expire, we used NULL for the expiration_date. This is perfectly acceptable when you don't have a value for every column, as long as the column allows NULL values.

There's another way to insert data that comes in particularly handy when you're copying information from one table to another. Let's say you're consolidating your pantry items with your spouse's inventory. You can use an INSERT statement combined with a SELECT:

```
INSERT INTO main_pantry (item_name, quantity, expiration_date)
SELECT item_name, quantity, expiration_date
FROM spouse_pantry
WHERE category = 'Non-perishable';
```

This query copies all non-perishable items from your spouse's inventory into the main pantry tracking system. The columns in the SELECT statement must match the structure of the columns you're inserting into, just like items need to fit on their designated shelves.

Sometimes you'll want to insert data while handling potential duplicates. Many databases support the INSERT OR IGNORE syntax (or similar variations depending on your database system). This is like checking if you already have an item before buying more:

```
INSERT OR IGNORE INTO pantry (item_name, quantity, expiration_date)
VALUES ('Flour', 1, '2024-10-15');
```

Some database systems use different syntax for this same concept. In PostgreSQL, for example, you might use ON CONFLICT:

```
INSERT INTO pantry (item_name, quantity, expiration_date)
VALUES ('Flour', 1, '2024-10-15')
ON CONFLICT (item_name) DO NOTHING;
```

You might also want to update existing records when inserting potentially duplicate data. This is commonly known as UPSERT (update or insert). In our pantry example, this would be like adding to the quantity if the item already exists:

```
INSERT INTO pantry (item_name, quantity, expiration_date)
VALUES ('Rice', 2, '2025-01-15')
ON CONFLICT (item_name)
```

DO UPDATE SET quantity = pantry.quantity + EXCLUDED.quantity;

When working with related tables, you might need to insert data that references other records. For example, if you're tracking recipes along with pantry items, you might insert recipe ingredients like this:

INSERT INTO recipe_ingredients (recipe_id, ingredient_id, amount, unit)

SELECT

(SELECT recipe_id FROM recipes WHERE recipe_name = 'Spaghetti Carbonara'),

(SELECT item_id FROM pantry WHERE item_name = 'Spaghetti'),

500,

'grams';

Error handling is important when inserting data. Many things could go wrong: duplicate keys, violated constraints, or invalid data types. It's good practice to wrap important INSERT operations in transactions:

BEGIN TRANSACTION;

INSERT INTO pantry (item_name, quantity, expiration_date)

VALUES ('New Item', 1, '2024-12-31');

—Check if the insert was successful

IF @@ERROR = 0

COMMIT TRANSACTION;

ELSE

ROLLBACK TRANSACTION;

When inserting large amounts of data, consider performance implications. Bulk inserts are generally more efficient than individual inserts. Many database systems offer specialized bulk import tools for large datasets. Also, if you're inserting many rows, consider temporarily disabling indexes and constraints, performing the insert, then re-enabling them.

Finally, it's crucial to validate data before insertion. Just as you wouldn't put spoiled food in your pantry, you shouldn't insert invalid data into your database. Consider creating triggers or using application-level validation to ensure data integrity:

```
CREATE TRIGGER check_expiration
BEFORE INSERT ON pantry
FOR EACH ROW
BEGIN
IF NEW.expiration_date < CURRENT_DATE THEN
SIGNAL SQLSTATE '45000'
SET MESSAGE_TEXT = 'Cannot insert expired items';
END IF;
END;
```

Remember that INSERT operations are permanent (unless rolled back), so always double-check your statements, especially when using INSERT with SELECT or when inserting multiple rows. It's good practice to test your INSERT statements with a small subset of data first, or use a transaction that you can roll back if needed.

By mastering INSERT statements, you'll be able to efficiently add new data to your database while maintaining data integrity and preventing errors. Whether you're adding single records or bulk-loading thousands of rows, understanding these concepts will help you manage your data effectively.

25. UPDATE: Modifying Your Address Book

Updating information in a database is much like revising your address book when friends and family move or change phone numbers. The UPDATE statement in SQL allows you to modify existing records, and knowing how to use it effectively is essential for maintaining accurate data.

Think about your address book. When a friend moves to a new house, you don't create a new entry - you modify their existing one. That's exactly what UPDATE does in SQL. The basic syntax is straightforward:

```
UPDATE contacts SET address = '123 New Street' WHERE first_name = 'John' AND last_name = 'Smith';
```

This command tells the database to find John Smith's record and change his address. The WHERE clause is crucial here - without it, you'd update every single record in your contacts table! It's like accidentally writing the same address for everyone in your address book. Always double-check your WHERE clause before executing an UPDATE statement.

Sometimes you need to update multiple fields at once. Perhaps your friend not only moved but also got a new phone number and email address. SQL handles this elegantly:

```
UPDATE contacts
SET
address = '123 New Street',
phone = '555-0123',
email = 'john.smith@email.com'
WHERE first_name = 'John' AND last_name = 'Smith';
```

You can also update values based on their current values. Let's say you're maintaining a loyalty points system, and you want to give everyone a 10% bonus on their current points:

```
UPDATE customer_rewards
SET points = points * 1.1
WHERE membership_status = 'Active';
```

The UPDATE statement becomes particularly powerful when combined with subqueries. Imagine you want to update all your business contacts with their company's new area code:

```
UPDATE contacts
SET phone = CONCAT('(555)', SUBSTRING(phone, 6))
WHERE contact_id IN (
SELECT contact_id
FROM business_relations
WHERE company = 'Acme Corp'
);
```

Sometimes you need to update records based on information in other tables. For example, updating customer status based on their recent purchase history:

```
UPDATE customers c
SET status = 'Premium'
WHERE EXISTS (
SELECT 1
FROM orders o
WHERE o.customer_id = c.customer_id
GROUP BY o.customer_id
HAVING SUM(amount) > 1000
);
```

When working with related tables, you can use JOIN in your UPDATE statement. This is particularly useful when you need to reference data from multiple tables:

```
UPDATE contacts c
```

```
JOIN companies comp ON c.company_id = comp.company_id
SET c.industry = comp.industry
WHERE comp.industry_updated = TRUE;
```

It's important to handle updates safely, especially when dealing with critical data. Using transactions is a good practice:

```
BEGIN TRANSACTION;
UPDATE bank_accounts
SET balance = balance - 500
WHERE account_id = '12345';
UPDATE bank_accounts
SET balance = balance + 500
WHERE account_id = '67890';
IF @@ERROR = 0
COMMIT TRANSACTION;
ELSE
ROLLBACK TRANSACTION;
```

You might also need to update records conditionally. The CASE statement comes in handy here:

```
UPDATE employee_records
SET salary =
CASE
WHEN years_of_service >= 5 THEN salary * 1.15
WHEN years_of_service >= 3 THEN salary * 1.10
ELSE salary * 1.05
END
WHERE department = 'Sales';
```

When updating large numbers of records, consider performance implications. Breaking up large updates into smaller batches can help:

```
DECLARE @BatchSize INT = 1000;
DECLARE @Processed INT = 0;
WHILE EXISTS (
SELECT 1
```

```
FROM contacts
WHERE processed = 0
)
BEGIN
UPDATE TOP (@BatchSize) contacts
SET processed = 1
WHERE processed = 0;
SET @Processed = @Processed + @@ROWCOUNT;
END
```

It's also crucial to validate data before updates. You can use CHECK constraints or triggers to ensure data integrity:

```
CREATE TRIGGER validate_email
BEFORE UPDATE ON contacts
FOR EACH ROW
BEGIN
IF NEW.email NOT LIKE '%@%.%' THEN
SIGNAL SQLSTATE '45000'
SET MESSAGE_TEXT = 'Invalid email format';
END IF;
END;
```

Remember to back up your data before performing significant updates. You can create temporary tables to test your updates first:

```
CREATE TEMPORARY TABLE temp_contacts AS
SELECT * FROM contacts;
UPDATE temp_contacts
SET status = 'Inactive'
WHERE last_contact_date < DATE_SUB(CURRENT_DATE, INTERVAL 1 YEAR);
—Review the results before updating the real table
SELECT * FROM temp_contacts WHERE status = 'Inactive';
```

Finally, it's good practice to verify your updates after execution. You can do this by selecting the updated records:

```
UPDATE contacts
SET status = 'VIP'
WHERE total_purchases > 10000;
SELECT * FROM contacts WHERE status = 'VIP';
```

By mastering UPDATE statements, you'll be able to maintain accurate and current data in your database. Whether you're updating single records or modifying thousands of rows based on complex conditions, understanding these concepts will help you manage your data effectively while avoiding common pitfalls like unintended updates or data integrity issues.

26. DELETE: Cleaning Out Your Garage

Just as we sometimes need to clean out our garage to remove items we no longer need, databases occasionally require cleaning up by removing unnecessary or outdated records. The DELETE statement in SQL provides a way to remove records from our database tables, but like cleaning out a garage, we need to be careful and methodical about what we remove.

Deleting records is one of the most powerful and potentially dangerous operations in SQL. Once data is deleted, it cannot be easily recovered without a backup. This is similar to throwing away items from your garage - if you accidentally dispose of something important, retrieving it could be difficult or impossible.

The basic syntax for deleting records is straightforward:

DELETE FROM garage_items WHERE last_used < '2020-01-01';

This command would remove all items we haven't used since before 2020. Notice the WHERE clause - it's absolutely critical. Without a WHERE clause, DELETE removes all records from the table, like emptying your entire garage in one go. Always double check your WHERE clause before executing a DELETE statement.

We can use various conditions in our DELETE statements. For example, removing duplicate items:

DELETE FROM inventory WHERE item_id NOT IN (SELECT MIN(item_id) FROM inventory GROUP BY item_name);

This would keep only one copy of each item, removing duplicates, much like keeping only one screwdriver when you find you've accumulated several over the years.

Sometimes we need to delete records based on their relationship to other data. For instance, removing all orders from customers who haven't made a purchase in two years:

```
DELETE FROM orders WHERE customer_id IN (SELECT customer_id FROM customers WHERE last_purchase_date < DATEADD(year, -2, GETDATE()));
```

When working with related tables, we need to be careful about referential integrity. If you have foreign key constraints, you might need to delete records in a specific order or use CASCADE DELETE options. This is like making sure you don't throw away a box that contains parts for something you're keeping.

For safety, it's often wise to begin with a SELECT statement to preview what will be deleted:

```
SELECT * FROM seasonal_decorations WHERE last_used < DATEADD(year, -5, GETDATE());
```

Once you've confirmed you're targeting the correct records, you can replace SELECT * with DELETE.

When dealing with large amounts of data, deleting records in batches can be more efficient and safer:

```
WHILE EXISTS (SELECT 1 FROM old_records WHERE processed = 0)
BEGIN
DELETE TOP (1000)
FROM old_records
WHERE processed = 0;
END
```

This approach is like cleaning out your garage one section at a time rather than trying to do it all at once, which can be overwhelming and risky.

For complex deletions, using Common Table Expressions (CTEs) can make your intentions clearer:

```
WITH OldItems AS (
SELECT item_id
FROM garage_items
WHERE last_used < DATEADD(year, -5, GETDATE())
```

```
AND condition = 'poor'
)
DELETE FROM garage_items
WHERE item_id IN (SELECT item_id FROM OldItems);
```

Sometimes you might want to archive data before deleting it. This is like putting items in storage rather than throwing them away:

```
INSERT INTO archived_items
SELECT *
FROM current_items
WHERE last_used < '2020-01-01';
DELETE FROM current_items
WHERE last_used < '2020-01-01';
```

Using transactions is crucial for maintaining data integrity, especially when deleting related records:

```
BEGIN TRANSACTION;
DELETE FROM order_details WHERE order_id = 12345;
DELETE FROM orders WHERE order_id = 12345;
IF @@ERROR = 0
COMMIT TRANSACTION;
ELSE
ROLLBACK TRANSACTION;
```

Some database systems offer soft deletes as an alternative to physical deletion. This involves adding a deleted_at timestamp or is_deleted flag rather than actually removing the record:

```
UPDATE items
SET deleted_at = CURRENT_TIMESTAMP
WHERE condition = 'broken';
```

This is like putting items in a "maybe" pile before deciding to permanently remove them.

When deleting based on complex conditions, subqueries can be very helpful:

```
DELETE FROM inventory
```

```
WHERE item_id IN (
SELECT i.item_id
FROM inventory i
LEFT JOIN usage_log u ON i.item_id = u.item_id
GROUP BY i.item_id
HAVING MAX(u.used_date) IS NULL OR MAX(u.used_date)
< DATEADD(year, -3, GETDATE())
);
```

Remember that some database systems provide additional safety features. For example, MySQL's LIMIT clause can restrict the number of rows deleted:

```
DELETE FROM old_records
WHERE created_date < '2020-01-01'
LIMIT 1000;
```

Finally, always ensure you have proper backups before performing major deletions. You might also want to script your deletions and test them on a copy of your data first:

```
CREATE TABLE temp_items AS SELECT * FROM items;
DELETE FROM temp_items WHERE condition = 'broken';
—Review results before applying to real table
```

By understanding these DELETE statement patterns and best practices, you can maintain clean and efficient databases while avoiding accidental data loss. Just like maintaining an organized garage, regular but careful cleaning of your database helps keep your data manageable and useful.

27. Table Creation: Building Your Dream House

Table creation in SQL is much like building your dream house. Just as you carefully plan each room's purpose, dimensions, and connections to other spaces, creating database tables requires thoughtful consideration of what data you'll store and how it will be structured.

Let's start with the basic blueprint. Creating a table begins with the CREATE TABLE statement, followed by the specifications for each column, much like defining the rooms in your house. Each column needs a name and a data type, just as each room needs a designation and specific features:

```
CREATE TABLE rooms (
room_id INT,
room_name VARCHAR(50),
square_footage DECIMAL(8,2),
floor_number INT,
windows INT
);
```

Think of data types as the fundamental characteristics of your rooms. Just as you wouldn't try to fit a king-size bed in a small closet, you need to choose appropriate data types for your data. VARCHAR is like a flexible space that can hold different amounts of text, while INT is more rigid, like a precisely measured room for specific purposes.

Constraints are like the building codes and structural requirements of your house. They ensure the integrity of your data, just as building codes ensure the safety and stability of your home. The NOT NULL constraint, for example, is like specifying that every house must have a front door:

```
CREATE TABLE house (
```

```
house_id INT NOT NULL,
address VARCHAR(100) NOT NULL,
bedrooms INT DEFAULT 3,
construction_date DATE,
last_renovation_date DATE
);
```

The DEFAULT constraint provides a standard value, like having a typical room size unless otherwise specified. This saves time when inserting new records, just as having standard room dimensions simplifies construction plans.

When creating tables that will store large amounts of data, consider the space requirements carefully. This is similar to planning storage spaces in your house. A VARCHAR(50) might be sufficient for a person's name, but you might need VARCHAR(1000) for detailed property descriptions. Using the appropriate size prevents wasting space while ensuring you have enough room for your data.

Tables often need to relate to other tables, just as rooms in your house connect through doorways and hallways. This is where we start thinking about primary and foreign keys, which we'll cover in more detail in upcoming chapters. For now, think of them as the connecting points between different parts of your database:

```
CREATE TABLE maintenance_records (
record_id INT,
house_id INT,
maintenance_date DATE,
description VARCHAR(500),
cost DECIMAL(10,2)
);
```

Sometimes you need to modify a table's structure after creation, just as you might need to renovate or expand your house. The ALTER TABLE statement allows you to add, modify, or remove columns:

```
ALTER TABLE house
```

```
ADD square_footage DECIMAL(10,2);
ALTER TABLE house
ALTER COLUMN address VARCHAR(200);
```

When creating tables, it's important to consider the future. Just as you might plan for a growing family when building a house, your database tables should accommodate potential growth and changes in requirements. This might mean including additional columns that you'll need later or choosing data types that allow for larger values than currently needed.

Temporary tables are like setting up a workshop while building your house. They exist only for a specific purpose and duration:

```
CREATE TEMPORARY TABLE construction_phase (
phase_number INT,
start_date DATE,
end_date DATE,
status VARCHAR(50)
);
```

Some database systems offer specialized table types for specific purposes. Partitioned tables, for example, are like building a house with different wings or sections, each optimized for specific uses. This can improve performance when dealing with very large datasets:

```
CREATE TABLE temperature_readings (
reading_time TIMESTAMP,
sensor_id INT,
temperature DECIMAL(5,2)
) PARTITION BY RANGE (EXTRACT(YEAR FROM reading_time));
```

When creating tables, naming conventions are like establishing a consistent addressing system for your neighborhood. Use clear, descriptive names that indicate the purpose of the table and follow your organization's standards. Avoid special characters and reserved words, just as you wouldn't use confusing or duplicate house numbers.

Documentation is crucial, just as keeping detailed blueprints of your house. Many database systems allow you to add comments to your table definitions:

```
COMMENT ON TABLE house IS 'Contains basic information about residential properties';
COMMENT ON COLUMN house.construction_date IS 'Original date of construction';
```

Consider the relationships between your tables carefully. Just as you wouldn't build a house without planning how rooms connect to each other, you need to think about how your tables will work together. This might involve creating junction tables for many-to-many relationships:

```
CREATE TABLE house_amenities (
house_id INT,
amenity_id INT,
installation_date DATE
);
```

Finally, always test your table design before loading it with data. Create sample records and verify that the structure meets your needs, just as you might create a model or detailed plans before building a house. Consider common queries and operations that will be performed on the table to ensure your design supports them efficiently.

Remember that while it's possible to modify table structures later, it becomes increasingly difficult as you accumulate data, just as major renovations become more challenging once a house is occupied. Taking time to plan your table structure carefully at the beginning can save considerable effort and complications later.

Through careful planning and consideration of these aspects, you can create table structures that efficiently store your data and support your application's needs, just as thoughtful house design creates functional and comfortable living spaces.

28. Primary Keys: Assigning Unique Student IDs

Primary keys are like assigning unique student IDs in a school system. Just as every student needs a distinct identifier to avoid mix-ups with records, grades, and schedules, every row in a database table needs a unique identifier to maintain organization and establish clear relationships between different pieces of information.

Think about your first day of school. The administration doesn't rely on names alone to identify students because multiple students might share the same name. Instead, they assign each student a unique ID number that will be used throughout their academic career. This number appears on report cards, class schedules, library cards, and any other school-related documents. Similarly, primary keys serve as the definitive identifier for each record in a database table.

A primary key must follow certain rules, just like student ID systems. First, it must be unique no one else can have the same identifier. Second, it cannot be null every student must have an ID number. These requirements ensure that we can always locate and reference specific records without ambiguity.

Let's consider how a school might structure its student database. The most straightforward approach is to use a simple numeric identifier:

```
CREATE TABLE students (
student_id INT PRIMARY KEY,
first_name VARCHAR(50),
last_name VARCHAR(50),
date_of_birth DATE,
grade_level INT
);
```

In this example, student_id is our primary key. The PRIMARY KEY constraint automatically enforces both uniqueness and the NOT NULL requirement. When new students enroll, the system ensures that each receives a unique identifier.

Sometimes, schools might use more complex systems for their student IDs. For instance, they might incorporate the year of enrollment or other meaningful information into the ID. However, the fundamental requirement remains the same: each value must be unique within the system.

Primary keys can also consist of multiple columns, known as composite primary keys. Consider a system tracking student attendance across different classes:

```
CREATE TABLE attendance (
student_id INT,
class_date DATE,
period_number INT,
PRIMARY KEY (student_id, class_date, period_number)
);
```

In this case, the combination of student_id, class_date, and period_number uniquely identifies each attendance record. No student can have multiple attendance records for the same class period on the same day.

Many database systems offer auto-incrementing primary keys, similar to a school automatically assigning the next available number when a new student enrolls:

```
CREATE TABLE students (
student_id INT PRIMARY KEY AUTO_INCREMENT,
first  name VARCHAR(50),
last_name VARCHAR(50)
);
```

Auto-incrementing keys simplify the process of adding new records because the database system handles the assignment of unique identifiers automatically. However, just as a school might need to consider special cases (like transfer students or returning students), your database design should account for various scenarios that might affect ID assignment.

Primary keys also serve as reference points for relationships between tables, much like how a student's ID connects their various school records. For example, when tracking grades, each grade entry would reference the student's ID:

```
CREATE TABLE grades (
grade_id INT PRIMARY KEY,
student_id INT,
subject VARCHAR(50),
grade_value DECIMAL(4,2),
FOREIGN KEY (student_id) REFERENCES students(student_id)
);
```

The choice of primary key can significantly impact your database's performance and usability. While simple numeric IDs are common, some situations might call for different approaches. For instance, a national student database might need to incorporate regional codes or other identifying information to ensure uniqueness across multiple schools.

When selecting a primary key, consider these factors:

- Stability: Will the value ever need to change?
- Size: Smaller keys generally perform better
- Meaningfulness: Should the key convey information, or simply serve as an identifier?
- Scalability: Will the key system accommodate future growth?

Just as a school must maintain its student ID system carefully to avoid duplicates or gaps, database administrators must manage primary keys thoughtfully. This includes planning for scenarios like merging databases, handling transferred records, or recovering from system failures.

Remember that primary keys are fundamental to database integrity. They're not just convenient labels; they're the foundation upon which reliable data relationships are built. Like a well-organized school system where every student's records can be quickly and accurately accessed, a database with properly implemented primary keys enables efficient data retrieval and maintains data consistency.

The impact of primary keys extends beyond simple identification. They enable complex queries, ensure data integrity, and form the basis for database relationships. Just as a student's ID connects their academic history, extracurricular activities, and administrative records, primary keys tie together different aspects of your data in a coherent and manageable way.

In the next chapter, we'll explore how foreign keys build upon this foundation to create meaningful connections between different tables, much like how family relationships connect different household members. Understanding both primary and foreign keys is essential for building robust and efficient database systems that can grow and adapt to changing needs while maintaining data integrity and accessibility.

29. Foreign Keys: Connecting Family Relations

Family relationships provide a perfect analogy for understanding foreign keys in databases. Just as we use birth certificates, marriage licenses, and other documents to formally establish family connections, foreign keys create official links between related data in different database tables.

Consider a family tree database. Each person has their own unique identifier (a primary key), but they also have connections to their parents, siblings, spouse, and children. These connections are established through foreign keys that reference the unique identifiers of related family members.

Let's explore how we might structure a simple family database. First, we need a table for individual family members:

```
CREATE TABLE family_members (
person_id INT PRIMARY KEY,
first_name VARCHAR(50),
last_name VARCHAR(50),
birth_date DATE
);
```

Now, to establish parent-child relationships, we create another table that uses foreign keys to connect children to their parents:

```
CREATE TABLE parent_child (
child_id INT,
parent_id INT,
relationship_type VARCHAR(20),
FOREIGN KEY (child_id) REFERENCES family_members(person_id),
FOREIGN KEY (parent_id) REFERENCES family_members(person_id)
```

```
);
```

Just as real family relationships come with certain rules and expectations, foreign keys enforce specific constraints to maintain data integrity. When you try to add a parent-child relationship, both the parent and child must already exist in the family_members table. This is similar to how you can't list someone as a parent on a birth certificate unless that person actually exists.

Foreign keys also help maintain consistency when data changes. If a family member's record needs to be updated (perhaps due to marriage and a name change), the foreign key relationships ensure that all connected records remain properly linked. This is similar to how updating a parent's name on their driver's license doesn't break their legal connection to their children.

The real power of foreign keys becomes apparent when we need to trace family relationships. For example, to find all of someone's grandchildren, we can follow the chain of foreign key relationships:

```
SELECT gm.first_name AS grandparent,
c.first_name AS grandchild
FROM family_members gm
JOIN parent_child pc1 ON gm.person_id = pc1.parent_id
JOIN family_members p ON pc1.child_id = p.person_id
JOIN parent_child pc2 ON p.person_id = pc2.parent_id
JOIN family_members c ON pc2.child_id = c.person_id;
```

Foreign keys also help maintain referential integrity, preventing orphaned records. Just as a child in the real world can't legally exist without parents, foreign key constraints ensure that every child_id in the parent_child table corresponds to an actual person in the family_members table.

We can extend this concept to other types of family relationships. Consider tracking marriages:

```
CREATE TABLE marriages (
marriage_id INT PRIMARY KEY,
```

```
spouse1_id INT,
spouse2_id INT,
marriage_date DATE,
FOREIGN KEY (spouse1_id) REFERENCES family_members(person_id),
FOREIGN KEY (spouse2_id) REFERENCES family_members(person_id)
);
```

These relationships can become quite complex, just like real family trees. You might need to track adoptions, step-relationships, or historical marriages. Foreign keys help maintain order in this complexity by ensuring that every relationship points to valid family members.

When designing tables with foreign keys, consider these important factors:

- Referential integrity: What should happen if a referenced record is deleted?
- Relationship cardinality: Can a child have multiple parents? Can a person be married to multiple people?
- Historical tracking: Do you need to maintain a history of relationship changes?

Foreign keys can include cascade rules that specify what happens when referenced records are modified or deleted. For example, you might set up rules so that if a person's record is deleted, all their relationship records are automatically removed:

```
FOREIGN KEY (child_id) REFERENCES family_members(person_id)
ON DELETE CASCADE
```

This is similar to how annulling a marriage might automatically void certain legal relationships that were established through that marriage.

Performance considerations are important when working with foreign keys. Just as looking up family relationships in paper records requires an organized filing system, databases need proper indexing on foreign key columns to efficiently query relationships:

```
CREATE INDEX idx_parent_child_parent ON parent_child(parent_id);
CREATE INDEX idx_parent_child_child ON parent_child(child_id);
```

Foreign keys aren't limited to just one reference column. Sometimes you need composite foreign keys that reference multiple columns, similar to how some legal documents might require both a person's ID number and their birth date to establish identity.

Understanding foreign keys is crucial for maintaining data integrity and building meaningful relationships between different types of information. They ensure that our data connections remain valid and traceable, just as legal documents and records maintain the official structure of family relationships in the real world.

In the next chapter, we'll explore how indexes help us quickly locate information in our database, much like a book's table of contents helps us find specific chapters without reading through the entire book.

30. Indexes: Creating a Book's Table of Contents

Just as a book's table of contents helps you quickly locate specific chapters without flipping through every page, indexes in databases serve as navigation tools that dramatically speed up data retrieval. Without indexes, finding information would require scanning through entire tables, much like searching for a specific recipe by reading through an entire cookbook.

Consider a large library with thousands of books. Without a catalog system, finding a specific book would mean checking every shelf until you found it. Libraries solve this problem by maintaining card catalogs and organizing books by categories, authors, and titles. Database indexes work in a similar way, creating organized reference points that help locate data quickly.

When you create an index, the database engine essentially builds a sorted list of values from the specified column, along with pointers to the full records where those values appear. This is similar to how a book's index lists important terms alphabetically, with page numbers telling you exactly where to find each reference.

Let's explore creating an index on a table of books:

CREATE INDEX idx_books_title ON books(title);

This command creates an index on the title column, allowing the database to quickly locate books by their titles. Without this index, searching for a book titled "The Great Gatsby" would require checking every single record in the books table.

Indexes are particularly valuable for columns that you frequently use in WHERE clauses or JOIN conditions. For example, if you often search for books by their ISBN number, creating an index on the ISBN column would significantly improve query performance:

CREATE INDEX idx_books_isbn ON books(isbn);

Now, when you run a query like SELECT * FROM books WHERE isbn = '978-0743273565', the database can quickly locate the matching record using the index instead of performing a full table scan.

You can create indexes on multiple columns, similar to how a library might organize books first by genre, then by author within each genre. These composite indexes are useful when you frequently search using combinations of columns:

CREATE INDEX idx_books_author_title ON books(author_name, title);

However, indexes come with trade-offs. While they speed up data retrieval, they require additional storage space and slow down insert and update operations because the index must be maintained as data changes. This is similar to how adding a new book to a library requires updating both the physical shelf organization and the card catalog.

Different types of indexes serve different purposes. The most common type is a B-tree index, which works well for equality comparisons and range queries. Hash indexes are optimized for exact matches but don't help with range queries. Some databases also support specialized indexes like full-text indexes for searching through large text fields.

When deciding which columns to index, consider these factors:

- Query patterns: Which columns appear frequently in WHERE clauses?

- Table size: Small tables might not benefit much from indexes

- Update frequency: Tables with frequent updates might suffer from too many indexes

- Uniqueness: Columns with many unique values often benefit more from indexing

Unique indexes serve a dual purpose: they both speed up searches and enforce data uniqueness. When you create a primary key, the database automatically creates a unique index on those columns:

CREATE TABLE customers (

customer_id INT PRIMARY KEY, —Creates an implicit unique index

name VARCHAR(100),

email VARCHAR(100) UNIQUE —Creates another unique index

);

Maintaining indexes requires regular attention, similar to how libraries periodically reorganize their collections. Over time, indexes can become fragmented as data is modified, leading to decreased performance. Database administrators need to monitor index usage and periodically rebuild indexes to maintain optimal performance.

You can view the indexes on a table using database-specific commands. In PostgreSQL, for example:

SELECT indexname, indexdef

FROM pg_indexes

WHERE tablename = 'books';

Understanding when NOT to create indexes is just as important as knowing when to create them. Indexes on columns that are rarely queried or have low selectivity (few unique values) might provide little benefit while consuming resources. For example, a column storing only 'Yes' or 'No' values probably doesn't need an index.

Some queries can use multiple indexes together to improve performance. This is like using both the library's subject catalog and author index to narrow down your search. However, the database engine must decide which indexes to use based on the specific query and available statistics.

Modern databases include query optimizers that decide whether to use available indexes based on various factors including table size, data distribution, and system resources. You can examine these decisions using EXPLAIN commands to see how your queries use indexes:

EXPLAIN SELECT * FROM books WHERE author_name = 'Jane Austen' AND publication_year > 2000;

Regular monitoring of index usage helps identify unnecessary indexes that can be removed and missing indexes that should be added. Many database systems provide tools to track which indexes are frequently used and which are sitting idle.

As your database grows, proper indexing becomes increasingly critical for maintaining acceptable performance. Without appropriate indexes, queries that once ran quickly can slow to a crawl as table sizes increase. This is similar to how a small personal library might work fine without a formal organization system, but a public library requires careful cataloging to remain usable.

Remember that indexes are not a "set and forget" feature. As your application's usage patterns change, you may need to adjust your indexing strategy. Regular review and maintenance of indexes, guided by actual query patterns and performance metrics, helps ensure your database continues to perform optimally.

31. CASE Statements: Making Situational Decisions

CASE statements in SQL are like the daily decisions we make based on different situations. Just as you might choose what to wear based on the weather, or which route to take to work depending on traffic conditions, CASE statements help databases make situational choices when processing data.

Think about planning a weekend activity. If it's sunny, you might go to the park; if it's raining, you might visit a museum; and if it's snowing, you might stay home. CASE statements follow this same logical pattern, evaluating conditions and providing different results based on which condition is met.

Let's start with a simple example using a customer loyalty program. Suppose you want to assign customer levels based on their annual spending:

```
CASE
WHEN annual_spend >= 5000 THEN 'Platinum'
WHEN annual_spend >= 2500 THEN 'Gold'
WHEN annual_spend >= 1000 THEN 'Silver'
ELSE 'Bronze'
END AS customer_level
```

This works just like how you might categorize your friends based on how often you see them. Those you meet weekly might be "close friends," monthly meetings indicate "good friends," and yearly encounters suggest "acquaintances."

CASE statements come in two forms. The first is the simple CASE expression, which compares a value against multiple possible matches:

```
CASE account_type
WHEN 'Savings' THEN 2.5
WHEN 'Checking' THEN 0.5
```

WHEN 'Money Market' THEN 3.0

ELSE 0.0

END AS interest_rate

The second form is the searched CASE expression, which we saw in the first example. This type allows for more complex conditions and different comparisons in each WHEN clause. It's like having a sophisticated decision tree for handling various situations.

You can use CASE statements in different parts of your SQL query. They're particularly useful in SELECT clauses to transform output, in WHERE clauses to create complex filtering conditions, and in ORDER BY clauses to create custom sorting rules.

For example, imagine sorting your task list based on priority levels that follow different rules for different departments:

SELECT task_name,

CASE

WHEN department = 'Sales' AND deadline <= CURRENT_DATE + 7 THEN 1

WHEN department = 'Support' AND status = 'Urgent' THEN 1

WHEN department = 'Development' AND complexity_level = 'High' THEN 1

ELSE 2

END AS priority_order

FROM tasks

ORDER BY priority_order;

CASE statements can also be nested, allowing for more complex decision trees. Think about choosing a vacation destination based on multiple factors like budget, season, and available vacation days:

SELECT destination,

CASE

WHEN budget >= 5000 THEN

CASE

WHEN season = 'Summer' THEN 'European Tour'

WHEN season = 'Winter' THEN 'Caribbean Cruise'
ELSE 'Domestic Resort'
END
WHEN budget >= 2000 THEN
CASE
WHEN vacation_days >= 7 THEN 'National Park Tour'
ELSE 'Weekend Getaway'
END
ELSE 'Staycation'
END AS vacation_plan

One powerful use of CASE statements is in calculating conditional aggregates. Suppose you want to analyze sales patterns across different seasons:

SELECT
COUNT(*) as total_sales,
SUM(CASE WHEN MONTH(sale_date) IN (12,1,2) THEN amount ELSE 0 END) as winter_sales,
SUM(CASE WHEN MONTH(sale_date) IN (3,4,5) THEN amount ELSE 0 END) as spring_sales,
SUM(CASE WHEN MONTH(sale_date) IN (6,7,8) THEN amount ELSE 0 END) as summer_sales,
SUM(CASE WHEN MONTH(sale_date) IN (9,10,11) THEN amount ELSE 0 END) as fall_sales
FROM sales;

CASE statements can also help in data cleaning and transformation. When combining data from different sources, you might need to standardize values:

SELECT
original_status,
CASE
WHEN original_status IN ('Y', 'yes', 'True', '1') THEN 'Active'
WHEN original_status IN ('N', 'no', 'False', '0') THEN 'Inactive'

```
WHEN original_status IS NULL THEN 'Unknown'
ELSE 'Review Required'
END AS standardized_status
FROM imported_data;
```

Remember that CASE statements evaluate conditions in order and stop at the first true condition. This is like following a decision flowchart: once you reach a valid answer, you stop and use that result. The ELSE clause provides a default value when none of the conditions are met, similar to having a backup plan when none of your preferred options work out.

You can also use CASE statements to pivot data, transforming rows into columns or vice versa. This is particularly useful for creating summary reports:

```
SELECT department,
SUM(CASE WHEN year = 2021 THEN budget ELSE 0 END) as budget_2021,
SUM(CASE WHEN year = 2022 THEN budget ELSE 0 END) as budget_2022,
SUM(CASE WHEN year = 2023 THEN budget ELSE 0 END) as budget_2023
FROM department_budgets
GROUP BY department;
```

CASE statements are also valuable in data validation and business rule implementation. You can use them to flag records that need attention:

```
SELECT order_id,
CASE
WHEN quantity > inventory_level THEN 'Insufficient Stock'
WHEN delivery_date < order_date THEN 'Invalid Dates'
WHEN amount < 0 THEN 'Negative Amount'
WHEN shipping_address IS NULL THEN 'Missing Address'
ELSE 'Valid'
```

```
END AS validation_status
FROM orders;
```

When using CASE statements, it's important to ensure that all possible scenarios are covered to avoid unexpected results. The ELSE clause serves as a safety net, but explicit handling of each important case makes your queries more maintainable and easier to understand.

Think of CASE statements as your SQL Swiss Army knife for handling conditional logic. They bring the power of if-then-else programming constructs into your database queries, allowing you to implement complex business rules and data transformations directly in your SQL code. Whether you're categorizing data, implementing business rules, or creating custom reports, CASE statements provide the flexibility to handle diverse scenarios in a clear and organized way.

32. String Functions: Formatting Names and Addresses

Working with text data in SQL is like organizing your address book or formatting names on party invitations. String functions give us powerful tools to manipulate text data, making it consistent and presentable, just like how we might standardize the way we write addresses on envelopes.

Let's start with a common scenario: names in a database often come in different formats. Some might be all uppercase, some lowercase, and others with inconsistent capitalization. The UPPER, LOWER, and INITCAP functions help us standardize this. Think of it like setting guidelines for how names should appear on official documents:

```
SELECT UPPER(last_name) as uppercase_name,
LOWER(email) as lowercase_email,
INITCAP(first_name) as properly_cased_name
FROM customers;
```

Just as you might need to combine a street address with a city and state, the CONCAT function (or the concatenation operator ||) helps join text together. Some databases use different syntax, but the concept is the same:

```
SELECT CONCAT(street_address, ', ', city, ', ', state, ' ', zip_code) as full_address
FROM addresses;
```

Sometimes addresses or names contain unwanted spaces, like when someone accidentally hits the spacebar twice while typing. The TRIM, LTRIM, and RTRIM functions help clean this up, just like how you might fix spacing errors in a document:

```
SELECT TRIM(both ' ' from name) as cleaned_name,
LTRIM(phone_number, '+1') as local_number,
RTRIM(email, '@oldomain.com') as username
```

FROM contacts;

When dealing with long text, you might need to extract specific parts, like getting just the street number from an address or the first few characters of a product code. The SUBSTRING function (sometimes called SUBSTR) handles this:

SELECT SUBSTRING(full_address, 1, 10) as address_start,

SUBSTRING(phone_number FROM 1 FOR 3) as area_code,

SUBSTRING(email FROM position('@' in email)) as email_domain

FROM customer_details;

Finding specific text within larger text is another common need. The POSITION or INSTR functions help locate substrings, like finding where an @ symbol appears in an email address:

SELECT email,

POSITION('@' IN email) as at_symbol_location,

INSTR(full_name, ' ') as space_location

FROM users;

Sometimes you need to replace certain text patterns, like updating old domain names in email addresses or standardizing state abbreviations. The REPLACE function handles this:

SELECT REPLACE(email, '@old.com', '@new.com') as updated_email,

REPLACE(state, 'California', 'CA') as state_code

FROM contacts;

When working with fixed-width fields, you might need to pad text to a certain length, like ensuring all product codes are 10 characters long. The LPAD and RPAD functions help with this:

SELECT LPAD(order_number, 10, '0') as formatted_order_number,

RPAD(product_code, 8, '-') as padded_product_code

FROM orders;

String functions can be combined to solve more complex problems. For example, extracting the username from an email address requires multiple steps:

```
SELECT LOWER(
SUBSTRING(
email
FROM 1
FOR POSITION('@' IN email) - 1
)
) as username
FROM users;
```

Working with names can be particularly challenging. Here's how you might split a full name into its components:

```
SELECT
SUBSTRING(full_name FROM 1 FOR POSITION(' ' IN full_name) - 1) as first_name,
SUBSTRING(full_name FROM POSITION(' ' IN full_name) + 1) as last_name
FROM contacts;
```

For handling special characters or patterns in text, regular expressions provide powerful capabilities, though the syntax varies between database systems. Here's an example of validating email addresses:

```
SELECT email,
CASE
WHEN email ~ '^[A-Za-z0-9._%+-]+@[A-Za-z0-9.-]+\.[A-Za-z]{2,}$'
THEN 'Valid'
ELSE 'Invalid'
END as email_status
FROM contacts;
```

String functions also help with data cleaning and standardization. Consider standardizing phone numbers:

```
SELECT
CASE
WHEN LENGTH(REGEXP_REPLACE(phone, '[^0-9]', '')) =
10
THEN CONCAT('(',
SUBSTRING(REGEXP_REPLACE(phone, '[^0-9]', ''), 1, 3),
') ',
SUBSTRING(REGEXP_REPLACE(phone, '[^0-9]', ''), 4, 3),
'-',
SUBSTRING(REGEXP_REPLACE(phone, '[^0-9]', ''), 7, 4))
ELSE 'Invalid Phone Number'
END as formatted_phone
FROM contacts;
```

When working with addresses, you might need to extract specific components:

```
SELECT
SUBSTRING(address FROM '^[0-9]+') as street_number,
REGEXP_REPLACE(
REGEXP_REPLACE(address, '^[0-9]+\s+', ''),
'\s+[A-Za-z]+,.*$', ''
) as street_name,
SUBSTRING(address FROM
'[A-Za-z]+,\s+[A-Z]{2}\s+[0-9]{5}$') as city_state_zip
FROM addresses;
```

Remember that string functions can impact performance, especially when used on large datasets or in WHERE clauses. It's often better to store pre-formatted data rather than applying string functions repeatedly in queries. Consider creating computed columns or maintaining standardized versions of frequently accessed text fields.

String functions make it possible to handle the messy reality of text data in our databases. Whether you're cleaning up user input, standardizing formats, or extracting specific information from text fields, these functions provide the tools you need to work with text data effectively. Just as we have conventions for writing addresses and formatting names in the real world, string functions help us maintain consistency and clarity in our database operations.

33. Date Functions: Planning Project Timelines

Managing dates and times in databases is like planning a complex project timeline, where you need to track deadlines, calculate durations, and understand the relationships between different time periods. Just as project managers use calendars and scheduling tools to keep everything organized, SQL provides powerful date functions to handle temporal data effectively.

Let's start with a common project management scenario: calculating how many days remain until a deadline. The DATEDIFF function (or equivalent, depending on your database system) helps us measure time intervals:

```
SELECT project_name,
deadline,
DATEDIFF(day, CURRENT_DATE, deadline) as
days_remaining
FROM project_tasks;
```

When planning project phases, we often need to add or subtract time periods. For example, if a task takes 30 days, we can calculate when it should start to meet the deadline:

```
SELECT task_name,
deadline,
deadline - INTERVAL '30 days' as must_start_by
FROM tasks;
```

Project timelines frequently involve working with different date components. Maybe you need to group tasks by month or find all deadlines falling in a particular quarter. The EXTRACT function helps break dates into their constituent parts:

```
SELECT task_name,
EXTRACT(month FROM deadline) as deadline_month,
```

```
EXTRACT(year FROM deadline) as deadline_year,
EXTRACT(quarter FROM deadline) as deadline_quarter
FROM project_timeline;
```

Sometimes we need to format dates differently for various stakeholders. Some might prefer MM/DD/YYYY, while others need YYYY-MM-DD. The TO_CHAR or DATE_FORMAT function (depending on your database) handles this formatting:

```
SELECT meeting_date,
TO_CHAR(meeting_date, 'MM/DD/YYYY') as us_format,
TO_CHAR(meeting_date, 'YYYY-MM-DD') as iso_format,
TO_CHAR(meeting_date, 'Month DD, YYYY') as long_format
FROM meetings;
```

Working with business days is crucial in project planning. You might need to exclude weekends when calculating task durations:

```
SELECT task_name,
start_date,
end_date,
DATEDIFF(day, start_date, end_date) as total_days,
DATEDIFF(day, start_date, end_date) -
2 * DATEDIFF(week, start_date, end_date) as business_days
FROM tasks;
```

Project managers often need to find the next occurrence of a particular day, like scheduling recurring team meetings every Monday:

```
SELECT meeting_name,
CASE
WHEN EXTRACT(dow FROM CURRENT_DATE) <= 1
THEN CURRENT_DATE + (1 - EXTRACT(dow FROM CURRENT_DATE))::integer
ELSE CURRENT_DATE + (8 - EXTRACT(dow FROM CURRENT_DATE))::integer
END as next_monday
FROM recurring_meetings;
```

Tracking milestone completion often involves comparing dates against current time:

```
SELECT milestone_name,
due_date,
CASE
WHEN due_date < CURRENT_DATE THEN 'Overdue'
WHEN due_date = CURRENT_DATE THEN 'Due Today'
WHEN due_date <= CURRENT_DATE + 7 THEN 'Due This
Week'
ELSE 'Upcoming'
END as status
FROM milestones;
```

Sometimes we need to work with fiscal years that don't align with calendar years. Here's how to calculate fiscal quarters:

```
SELECT
transaction_date,
CASE
WHEN EXTRACT(month FROM transaction_date) >= 7
THEN EXTRACT(year FROM transaction_date) + 1
ELSE EXTRACT(year FROM transaction_date)
END as fiscal_year,
CASE
WHEN EXTRACT(month FROM transaction_date) >= 7
THEN EXTRACT(quarter FROM transaction_date) - 2
ELSE EXTRACT(quarter FROM transaction_date) + 2
END as fiscal_quarter
FROM financial_transactions;
```

Working with timestamps across different time zones is another common challenge:

```
SELECT
meeting_time,
meeting_time AT TIME ZONE 'UTC' as utc_time,
```

```
meeting_time AT TIME ZONE 'America/New_York' as eastern_time,
meeting_time AT TIME ZONE 'America/Los_Angeles' as pacific_time
FROM global_meetings;
```

For reporting purposes, we often need to group dates into periods:

```
SELECT
DATE_TRUNC('month', activity_date) as month_start,
COUNT(*) as activities_count,
SUM(hours_spent) as total_hours
FROM project_activities
GROUP BY DATE_TRUNC('month', activity_date)
ORDER BY month_start;
```

When dealing with recurring events, we might need to generate a series of dates:

```
WITH RECURSIVE date_series AS (
SELECT start_date as series_date
FROM project_schedule
WHERE project_id = 1
UNION ALL
SELECT series_date + INTERVAL '1 week'
FROM date_series
WHERE series_date + INTERVAL '1 week' <= end_date
)
SELECT series_date
FROM date_series;
```

Date arithmetic can get complex when considering business rules. Here's how to handle holiday adjustments:

```
SELECT due_date,
CASE
WHEN due_date IN (SELECT holiday_date FROM holidays)
THEN due_date + INTERVAL '1 day'
```

```
WHEN EXTRACT(dow FROM due_date) = 0
THEN due_date + INTERVAL '1 day'
WHEN EXTRACT(dow FROM due_date) = 6
THEN due_date + INTERVAL '2 days'
ELSE due_date
END as adjusted_due_date
FROM deliverables;
```

Understanding and effectively using date functions is crucial for any database application that deals with time-based data. Whether you're tracking project progress, scheduling meetings, or analyzing historical trends, these functions provide the foundation for temporal data management. Remember that different database systems might use slightly different syntax for date operations, but the underlying concepts remain the same. Always consider time zones, business days, and fiscal calendars when working with dates to ensure your calculations align with business requirements.

34. Window Functions: Analyzing Sales Trends

Window functions in SQL are like analyzing sales trends over time, allowing us to see patterns and calculate running totals, rankings, and comparisons across different segments of our data. Just as a store manager might want to track sales performance across different periods or compare departments, window functions help us perform these calculations while maintaining the detail of individual records.

Let's start with a common retail scenario: calculating running totals of daily sales. Imagine wanting to see not just each day's sales, but also how sales accumulate throughout the month:

```
SELECT sale_date,
daily_sales,
SUM(daily_sales) OVER (ORDER BY sale_date) as running_total
FROM daily_sales;
```

This query shows both individual daily sales and their cumulative sum, helping identify trends and progress toward monthly targets. The OVER clause defines our "window" of data, in this case ordered by date.

Often, we want to compare performance across different store departments. The RANK and DENSE_RANK functions help identify top performers:

```
SELECT department_name,
monthly_sales,
RANK() OVER (ORDER BY monthly_sales DESC) as sales_rank,
DENSE_RANK() OVER (ORDER BY monthly_sales DESC) as dense_rank
FROM department_sales;
```

The difference between RANK and DENSE_RANK becomes apparent when there are ties. RANK might skip numbers (1,1,3), while DENSE_RANK keeps them consecutive (1,1,2).

Calculating moving averages helps smooth out daily fluctuations and reveal underlying trends. Here's how to calculate a 7-day moving average of sales:

```
SELECT sale_date,
daily_sales,
AVG(daily_sales) OVER (
ORDER BY sale_date
ROWS BETWEEN 6 PRECEDING AND CURRENT ROW
) as moving_average
FROM daily_sales;
```

Sometimes we need to compare performance across different regions while maintaining the detail level. PARTITION BY lets us create separate windows for each region:

```
SELECT region_name,
store_name,
monthly_sales,
SUM(monthly_sales) OVER (PARTITION BY region_name) as region_total,
monthly_sales / SUM(monthly_sales) OVER (PARTITION BY region_name) * 100 as percent_of_region
FROM store_sales;
```

Year over year comparisons are crucial for understanding business growth. We can use LAG or LEAD to compare current sales with previous periods:

```
SELECT sale_month,
monthly_sales,
LAG(monthly_sales, 12) OVER (ORDER BY sale_month) as last_year_sales,
```

(monthly_sales - LAG(monthly_sales, 12) OVER (ORDER BY sale_month)) /

LAG(monthly_sales, 12) OVER (ORDER BY sale_month) * 100 as yoy_growth

FROM monthly_sales;

For retail analytics, we often need to identify sales percentiles or quartiles:

SELECT product_name,

sales_amount,

NTILE(4) OVER (ORDER BY sales_amount) as sales_quartile,

PERCENT_RANK() OVER (ORDER BY sales_amount) as percentile

FROM product_sales;

Window functions can also help identify trends within specific categories. Here's how to find each product's rank within its category:

SELECT category_name,

product_name,

sales_amount,

RANK() OVER (PARTITION BY category_name ORDER BY sales_amount DESC) as category_rank

FROM product_sales;

Sometimes we need to calculate running totals that reset periodically, like monthly sales targets:

SELECT sale_date,

daily_sales,

SUM(daily_sales) OVER (

PARTITION BY EXTRACT(YEAR FROM sale_date),

EXTRACT(MONTH FROM sale_date)

ORDER BY sale_date

) as month_to_date_sales

FROM daily_sales;

Window functions can help identify sales anomalies by comparing each sale to nearby values:

```
SELECT sale_date,
daily_sales,
AVG(daily_sales) OVER (
ORDER BY sale_date
ROWS BETWEEN 3 PRECEDING AND 3 FOLLOWING
) as neighborhood_average,
CASE
WHEN daily_sales > 2 * AVG(daily_sales) OVER (
ORDER BY sale_date
ROWS BETWEEN 3 PRECEDING AND 3 FOLLOWING
) THEN 'Outlier'
ELSE 'Normal'
END as sales_pattern
FROM daily_sales;
```

For inventory analysis, we might want to track the first and last sales dates for each product:

```
SELECT product_name,
sale_date,
FIRST_VALUE(sale_date) OVER (
PARTITION BY product_name
ORDER BY sale_date
) as first_sale,
LAST_VALUE(sale_date) OVER (
PARTITION BY product_name
ORDER BY sale_date
ROWS BETWEEN CURRENT ROW AND UNBOUNDED
FOLLOWING
) as last_sale
FROM sales_history;
```

Window functions truly shine when analyzing customer behavior over time. Here's how to calculate days between purchases for each customer:

```
SELECT customer_id,
sale_date,
sale_amount,
sale_date - LAG(sale_date) OVER (
PARTITION BY customer_id
ORDER BY sale_date
) as days_since_last_purchase
FROM customer_sales;
```

These functions become particularly powerful when combined with other SQL features. For example, we can use them within CTEs or subqueries to build complex analytics:

```
WITH sales_stats AS (
SELECT product_name,
sales_amount,
AVG(sales_amount) OVER () as avg_sale,
STDDEV(sales_amount) OVER () as stddev_sale
FROM product_sales
)
SELECT product_name,
sales_amount,
CASE
WHEN sales_amount > avg_sale + 2 * stddev_sale THEN 'Exceptional'
WHEN sales_amount > avg_sale + stddev_sale THEN 'Above Average'
WHEN sales_amount < avg_sale - stddev_sale THEN 'Below Average'
ELSE 'Average'
END as performance_category
```

FROM sales_stats;

Window functions represent one of SQL's most powerful features for data analysis. They allow us to perform complex calculations while maintaining the granularity of our data, making them invaluable for sales analysis, performance tracking, and trend identification. While they might seem complex at first, thinking about them in terms of real-world business scenarios makes them more approachable and reveals their practical value in data analysis.

35. Temporary Tables: Creating Shopping Draft Lists

Temporary tables in SQL are like creating draft shopping lists before making your final version. Just as you might jot down items on a scratch pad while planning your grocery run, temporary tables provide a workspace to organize and manipulate data before reaching your final result.

Think about planning a large family gathering. You might start with several draft lists: one for groceries, another for decorations, and a third for seating arrangements. In SQL, temporary tables serve the same purpose, giving us a place to store intermediate results while working toward our final goal.

Let's start with a basic example. Imagine you're planning a party and need to track RSVPs. You might create a temporary table to manage the guest list as responses come in:

```
CREATE TEMPORARY TABLE party_rsvps (
guest_name VARCHAR(100),
response VARCHAR(20),
dietary_restrictions TEXT,
number_of_guests INT
);
```

This temporary table exists only for your current database session, disappearing when you're done, just like throwing away your draft shopping list after completing your purchases.

Sometimes we need to work with complex calculations in stages. Consider analyzing monthly sales data. Instead of writing one massive query, we can break it down using temporary tables:

```
CREATE TEMPORARY TABLE monthly_totals AS
SELECT
DATE_TRUNC('month', sale_date) as month,
```

```
SUM(sale_amount) as total_sales,
COUNT(DISTINCT customer_id) as unique_customers
FROM sales
GROUP BY DATE_TRUNC('month', sale_date);
```

Now we can easily reference these monthly calculations in subsequent queries without repeating the complex aggregation:

```
SELECT
month,
total_sales,
total_sales / unique_customers as average_customer_spend
FROM monthly_totals
WHERE total_sales > 10000
ORDER BY month;
```

Temporary tables are particularly useful when dealing with data transformations that require multiple steps. Consider preparing data for a customer analysis report:

```
CREATE TEMPORARY TABLE customer_activity AS
SELECT
customer_id,
COUNT(*) as total_purchases,
SUM(purchase_amount) as total_spent,
MAX(purchase_date) as last_purchase
FROM purchases
GROUP BY customer_id;
CREATE TEMPORARY TABLE customer_segments AS
SELECT
customer_id,
CASE
WHEN total_spent > 1000 THEN 'High Value'
WHEN total_spent > 500 THEN 'Medium Value'
ELSE 'Low Value'
END as customer_segment,
```

```
CASE
WHEN total_purchases > 10 THEN 'Frequent'
WHEN total_purchases > 5 THEN 'Regular'
ELSE 'Occasional'
END as purchase_frequency
FROM customer_activity;
```

Just as you might revise your shopping list several times before finalizing it, temporary tables can be updated and modified as needed:

```
UPDATE customer_segments
SET customer_segment = 'Premium'
WHERE customer_segment = 'High Value'
AND purchase_frequency = 'Frequent';
```

One powerful feature of temporary tables is their ability to simplify complex joins. Imagine analyzing product performance across different store locations:

```
CREATE TEMPORARY TABLE store_performance AS
SELECT
s.store_id,
p.product_id,
p.product_name,
COUNT(*) as units_sold,
SUM(s.sale_amount) as revenue
FROM sales s
JOIN products p ON s.product_id = p.product_id
GROUP BY s.store_id, p.product_id, p.product_name;
```

This temporary table now serves as a clean, aggregated dataset for further analysis:

```
SELECT
product_name,
SUM(units_sold) as total_units,
SUM(revenue) as total_revenue,
COUNT(DISTINCT store_id) as stores_selling
```

```
FROM store_performance
GROUP BY product_name
ORDER BY total_revenue DESC;
```

Temporary tables can also help when working with time-based analyses. Consider tracking customer purchase patterns:

```
CREATE TEMPORARY TABLE purchase_intervals AS
SELECT
customer_id,
purchase_date,
LAG(purchase_date) OVER (PARTITION BY customer_id ORDER BY purchase_date) as previous_purchase,
purchase_date - LAG(purchase_date) OVER (
PARTITION BY customer_id ORDER BY purchase_date
) as days_between_purchases
FROM purchases;
```

This setup allows us to easily identify customers who might need attention:

```
SELECT DISTINCT customer_id
FROM purchase_intervals
WHERE days_between_purchases > 90
ORDER BY customer_id;
```

When working with large datasets, temporary tables can improve query performance by storing intermediate results. Instead of repeatedly calculating the same aggregations, we can compute them once and store them temporarily:

```
CREATE TEMPORARY TABLE daily_metrics AS
SELECT
DATE_TRUNC('day', event_timestamp) as event_date,
COUNT(*) as total_events,
COUNT(DISTINCT user_id) as unique_users,
SUM(CASE WHEN event_type = 'purchase' THEN 1 ELSE 0 END) as purchases
```

```
FROM user_events
GROUP BY DATE_TRUNC('day', event_timestamp);
```

Remember that temporary tables are session-specific. When your database session ends, these tables are automatically dropped. This behavior is perfect for draft work that doesn't need to persist, just like throwing away your rough notes after finishing your shopping.

Some database systems also offer global temporary tables, which persist across sessions but contain session-specific data:

```
CREATE GLOBAL TEMPORARY TABLE session_cart (
item_id INT,
quantity INT,
added_time TIMESTAMP
) ON COMMIT PRESERVE ROWS;
```

This is similar to having a reusable shopping list template that gets cleared after each use but maintains its structure.

Temporary tables shine when preparing data for reporting. Instead of building complex views or maintaining permanent tables, you can create temporary tables that exist just long enough to generate your reports:

```
CREATE TEMPORARY TABLE report_data AS
SELECT
d.department_name,
e.employee_name,
p.project_name,
h.hours_worked,
h.date_worked
FROM hours_logged h
JOIN employees e ON h.employee_id = e.employee_id
JOIN departments d ON e.department_id = d.department_id
JOIN projects p ON h.project_id = p.project_id;
```

Think of temporary tables as your workspace for data analysis. Just as you might spread out your shopping lists, receipts, and budget calculations on a table while planning your monthly grocery shopping, temporary tables give you a place to organize, transform, and analyze your data before reaching your final results.

36. Data Import: Moving to a New House

Data import in SQL is like moving to a new house, where you need to transfer all your belongings from one place to another in an organized manner. Just as you carefully pack, label, and move your possessions, importing data requires thoughtful planning and execution to ensure everything arrives safely in your database.

Let's start with the basics of importing data from a CSV file, which is like moving boxes that have been neatly packed and labeled. Imagine you have a spreadsheet of your book collection that you want to import into your database:

```
COPY books(title, author, publication_year, genre, isbn)
FROM 'C:\my_books.csv'
DELIMITER ','
CSV HEADER;
```

This command tells SQL to take your neatly organized CSV file and place each item in its proper place in your database, just like unpacking boxes into designated rooms in your new home.

Sometimes your data might come in a slightly different format than your database expects, similar to furniture that doesn't quite fit through the door. In these cases, you'll need to make some adjustments during the import process:

```
COPY books(title, author, publication_year, genre, isbn)
FROM 'C:\my_books.csv'
DELIMITER ','
CSV HEADER
NULL AS 'unknown';
```

This tells SQL how to handle missing information, just as you might have a plan for dealing with items that don't have an obvious place in your new home.

When moving large amounts of data, it's often wise to do it in stages, just like you might move your essential items first and then gradually bring over the rest. Here's how you might import customer data in batches:

```
BEGIN;
CREATE TEMPORARY TABLE staging_customers (
customer_id INTEGER,
name VARCHAR(100),
email VARCHAR(255),
address TEXT,
phone VARCHAR(20)
);
COPY staging_customers FROM 'C:\customers.csv' CSV
HEADER;
INSERT INTO customers
SELECT * FROM staging_customers
WHERE customer_id NOT IN (SELECT customer_id FROM
customers);
COMMIT;
```

This approach is like using a staging area in your new house where you can organize items before placing them in their final locations.

Sometimes data needs to be transformed during the import process, similar to how furniture might need to be disassembled and reassembled when moving. Here's an example of importing and transforming sales data:

```
CREATE TEMPORARY TABLE raw_sales (
sale_date VARCHAR(50),
amount VARCHAR(20),
customer_info TEXT
);
COPY raw_sales FROM 'C:\sales_data.csv' CSV;
INSERT INTO processed_sales (sale_date, amount, customer_id,
customer_name)
SELECT
```

```
TO_DATE(sale_date, 'MM/DD/YYYY'),
CAST(REPLACE(amount, '$', '') AS DECIMAL(10,2)),
SPLIT_PART(customer_info, '|', 1),
SPLIT_PART(customer_info, '|', 2)
FROM raw_sales;
```

When dealing with data from different systems, you might encounter different formats, like moving between countries with different electrical systems. Here's how you might handle importing data from various sources:

```
CREATE OR REPLACE FUNCTION import_data(
source_type VARCHAR,
file_path VARCHAR
) RETURNS VOID AS $$
BEGIN
CASE source_type
WHEN 'csv' THEN
EXECUTE format('COPY target_table FROM %L CSV HEADER', file_path);
WHEN 'json' THEN
CREATE TEMPORARY TABLE json_import(data JSONB);
EXECUTE format('COPY json_import FROM %L', file_path);
INSERT INTO target_table
SELECT
data->>'field1' as field1,
data->>'field2' as field2
FROM json_import;
WHEN 'xml' THEN
—XML import logic
END CASE;
END;
$$ LANGUAGE plpgsql;
```

Large data imports can be time-consuming, like moving a large house full of furniture. It's important to monitor the process and handle any issues that arise:

```
DO $$
DECLARE
start_time TIMESTAMP;
rows_imported INTEGER;
BEGIN
start_time := CURRENT_TIMESTAMP;
CREATE TEMPORARY TABLE import_log (
batch_id SERIAL,
start_time TIMESTAMP,
end_time TIMESTAMP,
rows_processed INTEGER,
status VARCHAR(50)
);
—Perform the import in batches
FOR batch IN 1..10 LOOP
BEGIN
INSERT INTO import_log (start_time, status)
VALUES (CURRENT_TIMESTAMP, 'In Progress');
—Import batch
COPY target_table
FROM PROGRAM format('sed -n %s,%sp %s',
(batch-1)*1000 + 1,
batch*1000,
'input_file.csv')
CSV;
GET DIAGNOSTICS rows_imported = ROW_COUNT;
UPDATE import_log
SET end_time = CURRENT_TIMESTAMP,
rows_processed = rows_imported,
```

```
status = 'Complete'
WHERE batch_id = batch;
EXCEPTION WHEN OTHERS THEN
UPDATE import_log
SET status = 'Failed: ' || SQLERRM
WHERE batch_id = batch;
END;
END LOOP;
END $$;
```

Data validation during import is crucial, like checking for damage when moving valuable items:

```
CREATE TEMPORARY TABLE validation_results AS
SELECT
source_file,
COUNT(*) as total_records,
COUNT(*) FILTER (WHERE length(email) < 5) as invalid_emails,
COUNT(*) FILTER (WHERE amount < 0) as negative_amounts,
COUNT(DISTINCT customer_id) as unique_customers
FROM staging_table
GROUP BY source_file;
```

Finally, it's important to maintain a record of your imports, like keeping an inventory of moved items:

```
CREATE TABLE import_history (
import_id SERIAL PRIMARY KEY,
import_date TIMESTAMP,
source_file VARCHAR(255),
records_processed INTEGER,
success_count INTEGER,
error_count INTEGER,
import_duration INTERVAL,
```

```
notes TEXT
);
```

Just as moving to a new house requires careful planning, proper tools, and attention to detail, successful data imports depend on thorough preparation, appropriate methods, and diligent monitoring to ensure all your data arrives safely in its new home.

37. Data Export: Sharing Family Photos

Data export in SQL is much like sharing family photos, where you want to make your cherished memories accessible to others in a format they can easily view and appreciate. Just as you might choose different methods to share photos, whether through printed albums, digital files, or online galleries, SQL provides various ways to export data to meet different needs.

Let's start with the most common scenario: exporting data to a CSV file, which is like creating a photo album that anyone can open. Suppose you want to share your family's contact list with relatives:

```
COPY (SELECT name, phone, address, birthday FROM family_contacts ORDER BY name)
TO 'C:\family_directory.csv'
DELIMITER ','
CSV HEADER;
```

This command creates a neatly organized file that can be opened in any spreadsheet program, just like a photo album that any family member can flip through. The HEADER option includes column names, similar to adding labels to your photo album pages.

Sometimes you need to format your data in a specific way before sharing it, just like you might edit photos before printing them. Here's how you might export a formatted customer report:

```
COPY (
SELECT
UPPER(first_name) || ' ' || UPPER(last_name) as full_name,
TO_CHAR(join_date, 'Month DD, YYYY') as member_since,
CASE
WHEN total_purchases > 1000 THEN 'Premium Member'
ELSE 'Regular Member'
END as membership_status
FROM customers
```

WHERE active = true

) TO 'C:\active_members.csv' CSV HEADER;

When sharing sensitive information, you might want to exclude certain details, just as you might choose not to share certain personal photos. Here's how to export data while protecting private information:

COPY (

SELECT

order_id,

order_date,

total_amount,

SUBSTRING(credit_card_number, 13, 4) as last_four_digits

FROM orders

WHERE order_date >= CURRENT_DATE - INTERVAL '1 month'

) TO 'C:\recent_orders.csv' CSV HEADER;

Sometimes you need to export data in multiple formats, like sharing photos both digitally and in print. Here's a function that can handle different export formats:

CREATE OR REPLACE FUNCTION export_data(

export_format VARCHAR,

query_text TEXT,

output_path VARCHAR

) RETURNS VOID AS $$

BEGIN

CASE export_format

WHEN 'csv' THEN

EXECUTE format('COPY (%s) TO %L CSV HEADER', query_text, output_path);

WHEN 'json' THEN

EXECUTE format('COPY (%s) TO %L WITH (FORMAT JSON)', query_text, output_path);

```
WHEN 'xml' THEN
EXECUTE format('COPY (SELECT query_to_xml(%L, true, false, '''')) TO %L', query_text, output_path);
END CASE;
END;
$$ LANGUAGE plpgsql;
```

Large data exports can be resource-intensive, like processing a huge collection of high-resolution photos. It's often better to break them into manageable chunks:

```
DO $$
DECLARE
batch_size INTEGER := 10000;
total_records INTEGER;
num_batches INTEGER;
BEGIN
SELECT COUNT(*) INTO total_records FROM large_table;
num_batches := CEIL(total_records::FLOAT / batch_size);
FOR batch_num IN 1..num_batches LOOP
COPY (
SELECT *
FROM large_table
ORDER BY id
LIMIT batch_size
OFFSET (batch_num - 1) * batch_size
) TO format('C:\export_batch_%s.csv', batch_num) CSV HEADER;
END LOOP;
END $$;
```

Sometimes you need to transform data during export, like applying filters or effects to photos before sharing them. Here's how you might export sales data with calculated fields:

```
COPY (
```

```
SELECT
date_trunc('month', sale_date) as month,
department,
COUNT(*) as total_sales,
SUM(amount) as revenue,
AVG(amount) as average_sale,
STRING_AGG(DISTINCT cashier_name, ', ') as cashiers
FROM sales
GROUP BY date_trunc('month', sale_date), department
ORDER BY month, department
) TO 'C:\monthly_sales_summary.csv' CSV HEADER;
```

Scheduling regular exports is like setting up automatic photo backups. Here's how you might create a function for scheduled exports:

```
CREATE OR REPLACE FUNCTION scheduled_export() RETURNS VOID AS $$
DECLARE
current_file VARCHAR;
BEGIN
current_file := 'C:\exports\daily_report_' || TO_CHAR(CURRENT_DATE, 'YYYY_MM_DD') || '.csv';
COPY (
SELECT
current_date as export_date,
COUNT(*) as total_transactions,
SUM(amount) as daily_revenue,
COUNT(DISTINCT customer_id) as unique_customers
FROM daily_transactions
WHERE transaction_date = CURRENT_DATE
) TO current_file CSV HEADER;
—Log the export
INSERT INTO export_log (file_name, export_date, record_count)
```

```
SELECT
current_file,
CURRENT_TIMESTAMP,
COUNT(*)
FROM daily_transactions
WHERE transaction_date = CURRENT_DATE;
END;
$$ LANGUAGE plpgsql;
```

Just as you might want to maintain different versions of photos, you can export data with version control:

```
CREATE OR REPLACE FUNCTION versioned_export(
table_name VARCHAR,
version_number INTEGER
) RETURNS VOID AS $$
BEGIN
EXECUTE format(
'COPY (
SELECT *,
%L::INTEGER as export_version,
CURRENT_TIMESTAMP as export_timestamp
FROM %I
) TO %L CSV HEADER',
version_number,
table_name,
'C:\exports\' || table_name || '_v' || version_number || '.csv'
);
END;
$$ LANGUAGE plpgsql;
```

Finally, it's important to maintain proper documentation of your exports, just like keeping track of when and where you've shared your photos:

```
CREATE TABLE export_registry (
```

```
export_id SERIAL PRIMARY KEY,
file_name VARCHAR(255),
export_date TIMESTAMP,
record_count INTEGER,
file_size BIGINT,
export_format VARCHAR(50),
exported_by VARCHAR(100),
retention_period INTERVAL,
notes TEXT
);
```

Remember that like sharing photos, data export is about making information accessible while maintaining appropriate control over how it's shared and used. Always consider your audience's needs and capabilities when choosing export formats and methods.

38. Basic Database Design: Planning a Home Layout

Basic database design is much like planning the layout of a home, where every decision about space and organization affects how efficiently you can live in it. Just as you wouldn't build a house without a blueprint, you shouldn't create a database without proper planning. The way you arrange your furniture, designate rooms for specific purposes, and create storage solutions all have parallels in database design.

Let's start with the fundamental concept of identifying entities, which is similar to deciding what rooms you need in your house. Just as you might need a kitchen, bedrooms, and bathrooms, a business database might need tables for customers, products, and orders. Each entity represents a distinct concept that needs its own space and organization.

Consider a simple online bookstore database. First, we need to identify our main entities:

```
CREATE TABLE books (
book_id SERIAL PRIMARY KEY,
title VARCHAR(200),
author VARCHAR(100),
isbn VARCHAR(13),
publication_date DATE,
price DECIMAL(10,2)
);
```

This is like designing the library room in your house, with each book having its own specific place and characteristics. Just as you wouldn't store books in the kitchen, each piece of data belongs in its appropriate table.

Next, we need to consider how different entities relate to each other, much like how rooms in a house connect through doorways and hallways. In our bookstore example, customers can place orders containing multiple books:

```
CREATE TABLE customers (
customer_id SERIAL PRIMARY KEY,
first_name VARCHAR(50),
last_name VARCHAR(50),
email VARCHAR(100) UNIQUE,
phone VARCHAR(20),
address TEXT
);
CREATE TABLE orders (
order_id SERIAL PRIMARY KEY,
customer_id INTEGER REFERENCES customers(customer_id),
order_date TIMESTAMP DEFAULT CURRENT_TIMESTAMP,
total_amount DECIMAL(10,2),
status VARCHAR(20)
);
```

Just as you plan traffic flow in a house to prevent bottlenecks, you need to design relationships between tables that allow efficient data access. The connecting table between orders and books represents this flow:

```
CREATE TABLE order_items (
order_id INTEGER REFERENCES orders(order_id),
book_id INTEGER REFERENCES books(book_id),
quantity INTEGER,
price_at_time DECIMAL(10,2),
PRIMARY KEY (order_id, book_id)
);
```

Data integrity constraints are like the building codes of database design. Just as you wouldn't build a house without proper support beams, you shouldn't create a database without proper constraints:

```
ALTER TABLE books ADD CONSTRAINT positive_price
CHECK (price >= 0);
ALTER TABLE order_items ADD CONSTRAINT positive_quantity
CHECK (quantity > 0);
ALTER TABLE customers ADD CONSTRAINT valid_email
CHECK (email ~* '^[A-Za-z0-9._%+-]+@[A-Za-z0-9.-]+\.[A-Za-z]{2,}$');
```

Consider data types carefully, just as you would choose appropriate materials for different parts of your house. You wouldn't use carpet in a bathroom or hardwood in a shower:

```
CREATE TABLE inventory (
book_id INTEGER REFERENCES books(book_id),
warehouse_id INTEGER,
quantity INTEGER DEFAULT 0,
last_updated TIMESTAMP DEFAULT CURRENT_TIMESTAMP,
minimum_stock INTEGER DEFAULT 5,
maximum_stock INTEGER DEFAULT 100,
PRIMARY KEY (book_id, warehouse_id)
);
```

Indexing strategy is like planning access points to different areas of your house. Just as you need efficient ways to reach frequently used spaces, you need quick access to commonly queried data:

```
CREATE INDEX idx_books_isbn ON books(isbn);
CREATE INDEX idx_orders_customer ON orders(customer_id);
CREATE INDEX idx_orders_date ON orders(order_date);
```

Consider data volume and growth, like planning for future family expansion when designing a house. You might create partitioned tables for large datasets:

```
CREATE TABLE order_history (
order_id INTEGER,
customer_id INTEGER,
order_date TIMESTAMP,
total_amount DECIMAL(10,2),
status VARCHAR(20)
) PARTITION BY RANGE (order_date);
CREATE TABLE order_history_2022 PARTITION OF order_history
FOR VALUES FROM ('2022-01-01') TO ('2023-01-01');
CREATE TABLE order_history_2023 PARTITION OF order_history
FOR VALUES FROM ('2023-01-01') TO ('2024-01-01');
```

Documentation is like keeping the blueprints and maintenance records of your house. Create a data dictionary to track your database structure:

```
CREATE TABLE data_dictionary (
table_name VARCHAR(50),
column_name VARCHAR(50),
data_type VARCHAR(50),
description TEXT,
constraints TEXT,
last_modified TIMESTAMP DEFAULT CURRENT_TIMESTAMP,
modified_by VARCHAR(50),
PRIMARY KEY (table_name, column_name)
);
```

Consider security needs, like planning different levels of access in your home. Create roles and permissions accordingly:

```
CREATE ROLE store_manager;
GRANT ALL PRIVILEGES ON ALL TABLES IN SCHEMA public TO store_manager;
CREATE ROLE sales_staff;
GRANT SELECT, INSERT ON orders, order_items TO sales_staff;
GRANT SELECT ON books, customers TO sales_staff;
```

Finally, plan for maintenance and updates, just as you would plan for home maintenance:

```
CREATE OR REPLACE FUNCTION update_last_modified()
RETURNS TRIGGER AS $$
BEGIN
NEW.last_updated = CURRENT_TIMESTAMP;
RETURN NEW;
END;
$$ LANGUAGE plpgsql;
CREATE TRIGGER update_inventory_timestamp
BEFORE UPDATE ON inventory
FOR EACH ROW
EXECUTE FUNCTION update_last_modified();
```

Remember that good database design, like good home design, requires careful planning and consideration of both current needs and future growth. It's much easier to get things right from the start than to renovate later. Always consider the relationships between different components, ensure proper constraints and security measures are in place, and document your design decisions for future reference.

39. Normalization: Organizing a Library

Imagine walking into a disorganized library where books are scattered randomly across shelves, with multiple copies in different locations and inconsistent labeling. This chaos is exactly what database normalization aims to prevent. Just as a well-organized library makes it easy to find and maintain books, a normalized database makes data management efficient and reliable.

Normalization is like creating a logical shelving system for your library. Instead of having books randomly placed, you establish clear categories, eliminate redundancy, and ensure everything has its proper place. Let's explore this through a practical example of a small library database.

Consider a basic library tracking system that starts with a single, unnormalized table containing all information: book title, author name, author birth date, borrower name, borrower contact, checkout date, and return date. This is similar to having a single shelf where you pile everything related to books and lending. The problems become apparent quickly just as they would in a physical library using such a system.

First Normal Form (1NF) is like ensuring each book has its own clear entry on the shelf. In database terms, this means eliminating repeating groups and ensuring each cell contains only atomic values. Instead of listing multiple authors in one cell separated by commas, we create separate rows for each author-book combination. This is similar to how a library might use separate catalog cards for each author of a coauthored book.

Moving to Second Normal Form (2NF), we address partial dependencies. Think about how a library separates its author information from book information. There's no need to repeat an author's biographical information on every book card they've written. Instead, we create separate tables for books and authors, linking them through a logical system just as a library might use cross-reference cards.

Third Normal Form (3NF) takes us further by eliminating transitive dependencies. Consider how a library handles borrower information. Instead of writing a patron's full address on every checkout card, they maintain a separate patron database and simply reference a library card number. This same principle applies in database design where we separate borrower details into their own table.

Let's translate these concepts into practical SQL. Starting with our messy, unnormalized table:

```
CREATE TABLE library_records (
book_title VARCHAR(200),
author_name VARCHAR(100),
author_birthdate DATE,
borrower_name VARCHAR(100),
borrower_phone VARCHAR(20),
borrower_address TEXT,
checkout_date DATE,
return_date DATE
);
```

Through normalization, we create properly structured tables:

```
CREATE TABLE authors (
author_id SERIAL PRIMARY KEY,
author_name VARCHAR(100),
birth_date DATE
);
CREATE TABLE books (
book_id SERIAL PRIMARY KEY,
title VARCHAR(200),
isbn VARCHAR(13),
publication_year INTEGER
);
```

```
CREATE TABLE book_authors (
book_id INTEGER REFERENCES books(book_id),
author_id INTEGER REFERENCES authors(author_id),
PRIMARY KEY (book_id, author_id)
);
CREATE TABLE borrowers (
borrower_id SERIAL PRIMARY KEY,
name VARCHAR(100),
phone VARCHAR(20),
address TEXT
);
CREATE TABLE loans (
loan_id SERIAL PRIMARY KEY,
book_id INTEGER REFERENCES books(book_id),
borrower_id INTEGER REFERENCES borrowers(borrower_id),
checkout_date DATE,
return_date DATE
);
```

This normalized structure brings numerous benefits. Just as a well-organized library can quickly locate books, handle returns, and track availability, our normalized database can efficiently manage similar operations. When an author's information changes, we update it in one place rather than hunting through multiple records. When a borrower moves, we modify a single address rather than updating countless loan records.

However, normalization isn't about blindly following rules. Sometimes, like in a library's quick-reference section, you might deliberately denormalize for performance reasons. For instance, you might keep a count of available copies directly in the books table, even though it could be calculated from the loans table, to improve response time for availability checks.

The key is understanding the trade-offs. Full normalization provides data integrity and eliminates redundancy but can require more complex queries and joins. Selective denormalization can improve performance but introduces maintenance challenges. Just as a library might keep some frequently accessed reference materials in multiple locations for convenience, while maintaining strict organization for the main collection, database design often requires balancing theoretical purity with practical needs.

Consider also how normalization affects data maintenance. In a normalized database, adding a new book by an existing author is straightforward just as shelving a new book in a well-organized library is simple. You don't need to repeat the author's information; you simply reference their existing record. Similarly, when an author changes their name or a borrower moves, you update one record rather than hunting through the entire database.

Testing for normalization violations is like conducting a library audit. Look for repetitive information, update anomalies, and deletion anomalies. If deleting a loan record would lose the only copy of a borrower's address, you have a deletion anomaly. If updating an author's birth date requires changing multiple records, you have an update anomaly. These are signs that further normalization might be needed.

Remember that normalization is a tool, not a goal in itself. The ultimate aim is to create a database that serves its purpose efficiently and reliably, just as a library's organization system exists to help people find and manage books effectively. Sometimes, perfect normalization might not be the best answer, but understanding these principles helps you make informed decisions about when and how to apply them.

40. Transaction Management: Balancing a Joint Account

Managing financial transactions is much like keeping track of a joint checking account between spouses. When one person makes a deposit or withdrawal, it affects the shared balance, and both parties need accurate records. Transaction management in databases follows similar principles, ensuring that related changes happen completely and correctly or not at all.

Imagine you and your partner maintain a joint account. When you pay the monthly mortgage, several things need to happen: the payment amount must be deducted from your account, credited to the mortgage company, and your loan balance needs to be updated. If any part of this process fails, you need all steps to reverse, preventing partial or incorrect transactions.

In SQL, we handle these situations using transaction management. A transaction is a group of database operations that must be treated as a single unit. Let's explore this through a practical example of managing a joint bank account.

First, let's create a simple banking structure:

```
CREATE TABLE accounts (
account_id SERIAL PRIMARY KEY,
account_number VARCHAR(20),
balance DECIMAL(10,2),
last_updated TIMESTAMP
);
CREATE TABLE transactions (
transaction_id SERIAL PRIMARY KEY,
account_id INTEGER,
transaction_type VARCHAR(10),
amount DECIMAL(10,2),
```

```
transaction_date TIMESTAMP,
description TEXT
);
```

When transferring money between accounts, we need to ensure both the withdrawal and deposit succeed together. Here's how we might structure a transaction:

```
BEGIN;
UPDATE accounts
SET balance = balance - 500.00,
last_updated = CURRENT_TIMESTAMP
WHERE account_number = '1001';
UPDATE accounts
SET balance = balance + 500.00,
last_updated = CURRENT_TIMESTAMP
WHERE account_number = '1002';
INSERT INTO transactions (account_id, transaction_type, amount, transaction_date, description)
VALUES
(1, 'WITHDRAWAL', 500.00, CURRENT_TIMESTAMP, 'Transfer to Account 1002'),
(2, 'DEPOSIT', 500.00, CURRENT_TIMESTAMP, 'Transfer from Account 1001');
COMMIT;
```

The BEGIN statement marks the start of our transaction. Everything between BEGIN and COMMIT must succeed completely, or the database will roll back all changes, much like tearing up a check that was filled out incorrectly. This ensures account balances always remain consistent.

But transactions aren't just about simple transfers. Consider a more complex scenario where you're paying bills from your joint account. You might need to process multiple payments while ensuring you don't overdraw the account. Transaction isolation levels help manage how different operations interact with each other.

Transaction isolation levels are like the rules for balancing a checkbook when both partners are writing checks. The strictest level, SERIALIZABLE, is like requiring one person to finish all their entries before the other can start. More relaxed levels allow concurrent operations while preventing specific types of conflicts.

Here's how you might set an isolation level:

SET TRANSACTION ISOLATION LEVEL READ COMMITTED;

Different isolation levels protect against various phenomena:

- Dirty Reads: Reading uncommitted changes (like checking your balance while your partner's deposit is still processing)
- Non-repeatable Reads: Getting different results when reading the same data multiple times during a transaction
- Phantom Reads: When new rows appear in a range of records you're processing

Understanding deadlocks is crucial for transaction management. Imagine you and your partner both try to update the account balance simultaneously. Each person's transaction might wait for the other to complete, creating a standstill. Databases handle these situations with deadlock detection and resolution, typically by rolling back one transaction and allowing the other to proceed.

Error handling within transactions requires careful planning. Consider this example of a safe withdrawal:

BEGIN;

SAVEPOINT before_withdrawal;

UPDATE accounts

SET balance = balance - 1000.00

WHERE account_number = '1001';

SELECT balance FROM accounts WHERE account_number = '1001';

```
—If balance would go negative, roll back to savepoint
IF balance < 0 THEN
ROLLBACK TO before_withdrawal;
ELSE
COMMIT;
END IF;
```

SAVEPOINT creates a marker we can roll back to if needed, like having an eraser handy when balancing your checkbook. This allows for more granular control over transaction recovery.

Performance considerations are important when designing transactions. Long-running transactions can hold locks on database resources, potentially affecting other users. It's like keeping your checkbook for days while reconciling it – nobody else can make entries during that time. Keep transactions as short as practical while still maintaining data integrity.

Monitoring transaction health is similar to reviewing your monthly bank statement. Regular checks for long-running transactions, deadlock frequency, and transaction volume help identify potential issues before they become serious problems. Many database systems provide views or functions for transaction monitoring:

```
SELECT * FROM pg_stat_activity
WHERE state = 'active'
AND query_start < current_timestamp - interval '5 minutes';
```

Finally, remember that transaction management isn't just about preventing errors – it's about maintaining trust in your data. Just as you need to trust your bank statement's accuracy, applications need to trust their database's consistency. Proper transaction management ensures that trust is well-placed.

Through careful transaction management, we can ensure our database operations maintain the same level of reliability as a well-managed joint bank account, where every penny is accounted for and no operation is left half-complete.

41. Error Handling: Troubleshooting Recipe Mistakes

Just as following a recipe requires careful attention to catch and correct mistakes before they ruin a dish, proper error handling in SQL helps us gracefully manage unexpected issues in our database operations. When baking a cake, you might realize you're out of eggs halfway through or notice the oven temperature was set incorrectly. Similarly, databases need mechanisms to detect and respond to problems that arise during query execution.

Let's start with a common scenario in a recipe database. Imagine you're inserting new recipes, but need to ensure all ingredients exist in your ingredients table first. Without proper error handling, a missing ingredient could cause your entire application to crash. Here's how we might handle this situation gracefully:

We begin by wrapping our operations in a TRY-CATCH block (syntax varies by database system). This is like having a backup plan when cooking - if one step fails, you know exactly what to do next. For example, when adding a new recipe, we might check for existing ingredients, handle missing ones, and log any issues that occur.

Error handling isn't just about catching problems - it's about providing meaningful information about what went wrong and how to fix it. Think about following a recipe that simply says "if something goes wrong, stop." That's not helpful. Instead, we want specific guidance like "if the dough is too dry, add water one tablespoon at a time."

In SQL, we can create custom error messages that provide clear, actionable information. When validating recipe ingredients, we might want to specify exactly which ingredients are missing or invalid. This helps users understand and correct the issue quickly, rather than leaving them guessing about what went wrong.

Database constraints serve as our first line of defense against errors, like measuring cups prevent incorrect portions. For example, we might have a check constraint ensuring recipe serving sizes are positive numbers, or that preparation times can't be negative. When these constraints are violated, we need to catch and handle the resulting errors appropriately.

Error logging is crucial for maintaining a healthy database system. Just as professional kitchens keep records of problems and solutions, we need to track database errors for troubleshooting and improvement. A robust error logging system captures not just what went wrong, but also the context - what was being attempted, what values were involved, and when the error occurred.

Consider a scenario where we're updating recipe ratings. Multiple users might try to rate the same recipe simultaneously, potentially causing conflicts. Proper error handling ensures these conflicts are managed gracefully without losing data or corrupting our database state.

Sometimes errors occur because of temporary conditions, like network issues or resource constraints. In these cases, implementing retry logic can help overcome transient failures. This is similar to checking if an ingredient is available at another store before giving up on making a recipe.

Different types of errors require different handling strategies. Some errors, like unique constraint violations, might be expected and handled as part of normal operation. Others, like disk space errors, might require immediate administrator attention. Categorizing errors and defining appropriate responses for each category helps maintain system stability.

Error handling also includes validation of input data before processing. When adding a new recipe, we might verify that all required fields are present, numbers are within reasonable ranges, and text fields don't contain invalid characters. This preventive approach catches potential issues before they cause database errors.

In a production environment, error handling becomes even more critical. Users expect systems to handle errors gracefully and provide clear feedback. Nobody wants to see a technical error message - they want to know what went wrong in plain language and what they can do about it.

Performance monitoring can be integrated with error handling to detect and respond to issues before they become critical. For example, if query execution times start increasing, we might log warnings before actual timeouts occur. This proactive approach helps maintain system reliability.

Error handling should also consider security implications. When errors occur, we need to be careful about what information we expose to users. Internal database errors or stack traces might contain sensitive information that shouldn't be visible to end users.

Recovery procedures are an important part of error handling. Just as you might have instructions for salvaging an overcooked dish, databases need defined procedures for recovering from various error conditions. This might include rolling back transactions, cleaning up temporary data, or notifying administrators.

Testing error handling is as important as testing the happy path through your application. Create scenarios that trigger various types of errors and verify that your handling code responds appropriately. This might include simulating network failures, testing constraint violations, or verifying retry logic.

Finally, remember that error handling is not just about preventing system crashes - it's about providing a smooth, professional experience for users even when things go wrong. Well-designed error handling makes the difference between a system that gracefully handles problems and one that leaves users frustrated and confused.

By implementing comprehensive error handling in our database applications, we create robust, reliable systems that can handle unexpected situations while maintaining data integrity and user trust. Just as a well-equipped kitchen can handle cooking mishaps without ruining the meal, proper error handling ensures our database operations continue smoothly even when problems arise.

42. Performance Tuning: Optimizing Your Daily Routine

Just as we look for ways to streamline our daily routines to save time and energy, database performance tuning helps our queries run faster and more efficiently. Think about how you might reorganize your morning routine to get to work on time - maybe you lay out your clothes the night before, prep your coffee maker, or find a faster route to the office. Similarly, we can optimize our database queries to work smarter, not harder.

Let's start with a common scenario many of us face: searching through email. When you have thousands of emails, finding a specific message can take forever if you're looking through them one by one. But with proper indexing and efficient search terms, you can locate what you need instantly. Database queries work the same way - without optimization, they might scan entire tables unnecessarily when they could use indexes to jump straight to the relevant data.

Consider how you might organize your kitchen to cook more efficiently. Frequently used items are kept within easy reach, while holiday serving platters might be stored up high. This is similar to how we structure database tables and indexes. Frequently accessed data should be easy to retrieve, while less commonly used information can be stored in ways that prioritize space efficiency over access speed.

One of the first steps in performance tuning is analyzing query execution plans - think of this like reviewing your grocery shopping route through the store. Are you zigzagging back and forth between aisles, or moving efficiently from one section to the next? Query execution plans show us how the database engine is accessing and processing data, helping us identify inefficient patterns.

Just as you might batch similar errands together to save time, we can optimize queries by combining related operations. Instead of making multiple trips to the database, we might use joins or subqueries to gather all needed information in a single request. However, like planning too many errands at once, overly complex queries can sometimes be less efficient than simpler alternatives.

Proper indexing is perhaps the most powerful tool for performance tuning. It's similar to having a well-organized filing system - when you need a specific document, you don't want to search through every folder. Instead, you use labels, categories, and alphabetical ordering to quickly locate what you need. Database indexes work the same way, providing shortcuts to locate data without scanning entire tables.

Sometimes performance issues arise from how data is stored. Just as you might reorganize your closet seasonally, databases sometimes need maintenance to maintain optimal performance. This might involve rebuilding indexes, updating statistics, or reorganizing table data to eliminate fragmentation.

Memory management plays a crucial role in database performance. Think about cooking in a tiny kitchen - you need to be strategic about counter space and which utensils you keep readily available. Similarly, databases need to manage memory efficiently, keeping frequently accessed data in memory while properly handling less frequently used information.

Query optimization often involves finding the right balance between competing needs. Just as you might choose between taking a longer route with less traffic or a shorter route through congestion, sometimes we need to balance different approaches to data access. The "best" solution often depends on specific circumstances and requirements.

Understanding and using statistics is crucial for performance tuning. The database engine uses statistics about your data to make decisions about how to execute queries - similar to how you might check traffic patterns to plan your commute. Keeping these statistics up to date helps ensure the database makes optimal choices.

Sometimes performance issues aren't about the queries themselves but about concurrency - how well the database handles multiple users or operations simultaneously. This is like managing a busy kitchen where multiple cooks need to work efficiently without getting in each other's way. Proper concurrency management ensures resources are used effectively while maintaining data integrity.

Caching frequently accessed data can dramatically improve performance, much like keeping commonly used ingredients on your kitchen counter instead of in the pantry. However, like food freshness, we need to ensure cached data doesn't become stale and that we're not using too much memory for caching at the expense of other operations.

Performance tuning isn't just about making things faster - it's also about resource efficiency. A faster query that consumes excessive server resources might not be the best solution, just as taking your own car might be faster but less efficient than using public transportation for your commute.

Regular monitoring and maintenance are essential for maintaining good performance. Just as you might track your monthly expenses to identify areas for improvement, monitoring database performance helps identify potential issues before they become serious problems. This includes watching for trends in query execution times, resource usage, and user activity patterns.

Sometimes the best performance improvements come from rethinking our approach entirely. Instead of trying to optimize a complex query, we might redesign our data model or change how we store and access information. This is similar to realizing that reorganizing your entire kitchen layout might be more effective than just rearranging items in existing cabinets.

By approaching performance tuning with the same practical mindset we use to optimize our daily routines, we can significantly improve database efficiency and responsiveness. Remember that optimization is an ongoing process - as our data grows and usage patterns change, we need to continuously monitor and adjust our approach to maintain optimal performance.

43. Security Basics: Protecting Your Home

Just as we take precautions to protect our homes and valuables, database security requires thoughtful measures to safeguard sensitive information. Think about how you secure your house - you lock doors, install security systems, and carefully choose who gets spare keys. Database security follows similar principles, creating layers of protection to keep data safe while ensuring authorized users can still access what they need.

Let's start with the foundation of database security: authentication and authorization. When you host a party at your home, you first verify who people are at the door (authentication) and then decide which areas of your house they can access (authorization). In database terms, authentication ensures users are who they claim to be, typically through usernames and passwords, while authorization determines what actions they can perform once logged in.

Consider how you might handle different visitors to your home. Family members might have keys to every room, while housekeepers might only access certain areas during specific hours. Database permissions work similarly. Some users might need full access to modify data, while others should only view specific information. Just as you wouldn't give every visitor unrestricted access to your home, not every database user needs complete system access.

Encryption plays a crucial role in database security, much like how you might use a safe for valuable documents. Even if someone manages to break in, encrypted data remains unreadable without the proper keys. Modern databases offer various encryption options, both for data at rest (stored in the database) and data in transit (being transmitted between systems).

Regular security audits are essential, similar to periodically checking your home's locks, windows, and security systems. These audits help identify potential vulnerabilities before they can be exploited. Just as you might notice a broken window lock during a home inspection, security audits can reveal database configuration issues or suspicious access patterns.

Backup security is often overlooked but critically important. Think about how you protect copies of important documents - perhaps keeping them in a safety deposit box or with a trusted relative. Similarly, database backups need protection to prevent unauthorized access while ensuring they're available when needed for recovery.

User management requires ongoing attention, much like maintaining a list of who has keys to your house. When someone moves out or changes roles, you update their access accordingly. Database user accounts need similar maintenance - removing accounts when people leave, updating permissions when roles change, and regularly reviewing access rights to ensure they remain appropriate.

Password policies play a crucial role in security, similar to choosing strong locks for your doors. Just as you wouldn't use a flimsy lock on your front door, databases need robust password requirements to prevent unauthorized access. This includes minimum length requirements, complexity rules, and regular password changes.

Network security forms another crucial layer of protection. Think about how your home's security extends beyond just locks - you might have exterior lighting, security cameras, or a gated community. Similarly, databases need network-level protection through firewalls, secure protocols, and careful configuration of remote access options.

Security logging and monitoring are like having security cameras for your database. Just as you might review security footage after a suspicious incident, database logs help track who accessed what data and when. This information proves invaluable for investigating security incidents and maintaining compliance with privacy regulations.

Data masking and redaction protect sensitive information, similar to how you might cover personal information on documents before sharing them. When providing data for testing or reporting, sensitive details can be obscured while maintaining the data's overall structure and usefulness.

Role-based access control organizes permissions efficiently, much like how you might organize house keys for different types of visitors. Instead of managing individual permissions for each user, roles group common access needs together. This makes security management more straightforward while reducing the risk of permission errors.

Understanding and implementing security best practices requires balancing protection with usability. Just as overly complicated home security might discourage family visits, excessive security measures can make databases difficult to use effectively. The goal is finding the right balance between security and accessibility.

Regular security training helps users understand their role in maintaining database security, similar to teaching family members about home security practices. Users need to understand why security measures exist and how to follow them properly. This includes password management, handling sensitive data, and recognizing potential security threats.

Incident response planning prepares for security breaches, much like having a plan for home emergencies. Knowing what to do if security is compromised helps minimize damage and restore normal operations quickly. This includes procedures for identifying breaches, containing damage, and recovering affected systems.

By approaching database security with the same careful consideration we give to protecting our homes, we can create effective layers of protection while maintaining necessary access. Remember that security is an ongoing process requiring regular attention and updates as threats and requirements evolve.

44. Backup and Recovery: Creating Family Photo Albums

Think of database backup and recovery like creating and preserving family photo albums. Just as we carefully store and protect precious memories, databases need systematic backup procedures to safeguard valuable information. The process involves regular snapshots of data, secure storage, and reliable methods to restore information when needed.

Creating database backups follows a rhythm similar to how we organize family photos. Some photos we back up immediately after important events, while others we archive periodically as part of our regular routine. Similarly, database backups follow different schedules and strategies depending on the data's importance and how frequently it changes. Full backups capture everything at once, like creating a complete family photo album, while incremental backups only store what's changed since the last backup, similar to adding new photos to an existing album.

The choice of backup timing and frequency depends on how much data you can afford to lose in a worst case scenario. Consider how devastating it would be to lose photos from a wedding versus everyday snapshots. Critical business databases might require constant backups, while less crucial systems might only need daily or weekly backups. This concept, known as the Recovery Point Objective (RPO), helps determine appropriate backup schedules.

Storage location matters as much as the backup process itself. Just as you wouldn't keep your only copy of irreplaceable family photos in the same house as the originals, database backups should be stored in separate physical locations. Cloud storage, offsite facilities, and geographically distributed backup systems provide protection against local disasters. The key is ensuring backups remain accessible while being sufficiently separated from the primary data.

Testing backup integrity proves just as important as creating the backups themselves. Like discovering a corrupted photo file when trying to print an old picture, an untested backup might fail when needed most. Regular restoration tests verify that backups remain viable and that recovery procedures work as expected. These tests also help teams practice recovery procedures, ensuring they can act quickly during actual emergencies.

Recovery strategies need careful planning, much like organizing a systematic way to find specific photos in your collection. When data loss occurs, having clear procedures helps restore information quickly and accurately. This includes knowing which backup to use, understanding the restoration process, and having documented steps for different recovery scenarios. The time required to restore operations, known as the Recovery Time Objective (RTO), guides these planning decisions.

Different types of backups serve different purposes, similar to how we might keep multiple versions of important photos. Full backups provide complete point in time copies but require more storage space and time to create. Differential backups store changes since the last full backup, while incremental backups record changes since the most recent backup of any type. Each approach balances storage requirements, backup time, and recovery complexity.

Security remains crucial throughout the backup process. Just as you wouldn't leave precious family photos unprotected, database backups need encryption and access controls. Backup files often contain complete copies of sensitive information, making them attractive targets for unauthorized access. Proper security measures protect backup data both during creation and in storage.

Automation plays a vital role in reliable backup systems. Like using automatic cloud backup for your phone's photos, database backups should run automatically on schedule. This removes human error from the process and ensures consistent execution. Automated systems can also verify backup completion and alert administrators to any problems.

Retention policies determine how long to keep different backups, similar to deciding which photos to preserve long term. Some backups might need retention for years due to regulatory requirements or business needs, while others can be cycled out more quickly. Clear policies help manage storage space while ensuring necessary historical data remains available.

Disaster recovery planning extends beyond simple backups to address major system failures. Think of it like having a plan to preserve and restore family photos after a house fire. This includes maintaining documentation of system configurations, understanding dependencies between different components, and having procedures to rebuild entire systems if necessary.

Version control for backup systems helps track changes and ensure consistency. Just as you might note when and how photo albums were organized, maintaining records of backup procedures and configurations helps troubleshoot problems and maintain system reliability. This documentation proves especially valuable when recovering from complex failures or when new team members need to understand the backup system.

Cost considerations influence backup strategies, balancing protection against resource usage. Like choosing between different photo storage options, organizations must weigh factors like storage costs, bandwidth usage, and administrative overhead. Cloud backup services offer flexibility but may incur ongoing costs, while local storage requires upfront investment in hardware and maintenance.

Modern backup systems often integrate with cloud services, providing additional layers of protection and accessibility. Similar to how cloud photo storage offers automatic backup and sharing capabilities, cloud database backups can provide geographical distribution, automatic scaling, and simplified management. However, careful attention to security and privacy remains essential when using cloud services.

The future of backup and recovery continues evolving with new technologies and changing needs. Just as digital photos have transformed how we preserve memories, emerging technologies like artificial intelligence and automated recovery systems are changing how we protect and restore data. Understanding these advances while maintaining focus on fundamental backup principles helps organizations adapt while ensuring reliable data protection.

45. Working with Large Datasets: Managing a Warehouse

Managing large datasets shares many similarities with running a warehouse operation. Just as warehouse managers must efficiently organize, track, and access thousands of items, database professionals need strategies for handling millions or billions of records while maintaining performance and usability.

Consider how a warehouse organizes items into logical sections, uses clear labeling systems, and maintains efficient paths for retrieving products. Similarly, when working with large datasets, proper table partitioning divides data into manageable chunks. For example, a retail database might partition sales records by date ranges, making it easier to access recent transactions while maintaining historical data in less frequently accessed partitions.

Storage optimization becomes crucial when dealing with large volumes of data. Like maximizing warehouse space by choosing appropriate shelving and storage solutions, database professionals must select suitable data types and compression methods. Using the smallest appropriate data type for each column, implementing row or page compression, and regularly archiving old data helps manage storage requirements while maintaining performance.

Efficient indexing strategies prove essential for large datasets, much like how a warehouse needs well organized inventory systems. However, too many indexes can slow down write operations and consume excessive storage, similar to how too many inventory tracking systems might actually reduce warehouse efficiency. The key lies in identifying the most common access patterns and creating targeted indexes to support them.

Query optimization takes on greater importance with large datasets. Just as a warehouse needs efficient picking routes to fulfill orders quickly, queries need careful construction to minimize resource usage. This includes techniques like avoiding SELECT *, using appropriate JOIN strategies, and leveraging index coverage. Understanding query execution plans helps identify performance bottlenecks, similar to analyzing warehouse workflow patterns to improve efficiency.

Batch processing often provides the most efficient way to handle large scale data operations. Like how warehouses process incoming shipments in batches rather than individual items, database operations on large datasets benefit from grouped processing. This might involve breaking large updates into manageable chunks, using bulk insert operations, or implementing staged data loading processes.

Memory management requires careful attention when working with large datasets. Just as a warehouse needs adequate staging areas for processing shipments, databases need sufficient memory for query execution. Understanding concepts like memory grants, spill to disk operations, and buffer pool management helps prevent performance problems caused by memory pressure.

Parallel processing capabilities become increasingly important as data volumes grow. Similar to how large warehouses employ multiple workers to process orders simultaneously, modern database systems can leverage multiple processor cores for parallel query execution. However, proper configuration proves essential to prevent resource contention and ensure efficient workload distribution.

Data archival strategies help manage growing datasets while maintaining system performance. Like how warehouses might move seasonal items to long term storage, databases can migrate older data to separate archive tables or databases. This approach maintains data accessibility while reducing the active dataset size and improving query performance on current data.

Monitoring and maintenance take on greater importance with large datasets. Just as warehouse managers track inventory levels, space utilization, and operation efficiency, database administrators need comprehensive monitoring of storage usage, query performance, and system resources. Regular maintenance activities like statistics updates, index maintenance, and storage cleanup become critical for sustained performance.

Error handling requires robust strategies when dealing with large datasets. Like how warehouses need procedures for handling damaged shipments or inventory discrepancies, database operations need reliable error handling and recovery procedures. This includes implementing checkpoints during long running operations, maintaining transaction logs, and having procedures for handling partial failures.

Data quality management presents unique challenges with large datasets. Similar to how warehouses must maintain accurate inventory counts across thousands of items, ensuring data accuracy and consistency across millions of records requires systematic approaches. This might include automated validation rules, regular data quality checks, and procedures for correcting identified issues.

Security considerations scale with data volume. Just as larger warehouses need more sophisticated security systems, databases containing large amounts of sensitive information require comprehensive security measures. This includes fine grained access controls, audit logging, and encryption for data both at rest and in transit.

Performance testing becomes more complex with large datasets. Like how warehouse systems need testing under full load conditions, database systems require thorough testing with realistic data volumes. This includes load testing, stress testing, and monitoring system behavior under various operational scenarios.

Scalability planning ensures systems can handle growing data volumes. Similar to how warehouses plan for expansion, database systems need architectural approaches that support growth. This might involve implementing distributed databases, planning for hardware upgrades, or designing for cloud scaling capabilities.

Documentation and procedures become increasingly important as data volumes grow. Like how large warehouses need clear operational procedures, managing large datasets requires comprehensive documentation of data structures, maintenance procedures, and operational practices. This documentation helps ensure consistent operations and supports knowledge transfer between team members.

46. Analyzing Customer Behavior: Understanding Shopping Patterns

Understanding customer behavior through data analysis shares many parallels with being an attentive shopkeeper who remembers their regular customers' preferences and shopping patterns. Just as a local store owner might notice that Mrs. Johnson always buys fresh bread on Wednesdays or that Mr. Thompson tends to stock up on coffee when it's on sale, SQL allows us to systematically analyze and understand customer behavior at scale.

Let's start with the basics of tracking customer purchases. A simple query might look at frequency of visits, much like noting how often someone comes to your store. We can use COUNT and GROUP BY functions to see how many transactions each customer makes per month. This helps identify your most loyal customers, similar to recognizing familiar faces at a neighborhood shop.

Understanding what products customers typically buy together resembles observing shopping cart combinations at checkout. Using JOIN operations between transaction and product tables, along with window functions, we can analyze which items are frequently purchased together. This is like noticing that customers who buy pasta often pick up tomato sauce as well, but at a much larger scale.

Seasonal patterns emerge through careful analysis of transaction dates. Just as a store owner notices increased ice cream sales during summer months, we can use date functions and aggregations to identify seasonal trends. This might involve looking at sales volumes by month, day of week, or even time of day to optimize inventory and staffing levels.

Customer segmentation through SQL helps organize customers into meaningful groups, much like mentally categorizing your regulars. Using CASE statements and aggregate functions, we can segment customers based on various criteria such as purchase frequency, average transaction value, or product preferences. This helps tailor marketing efforts and inventory decisions to different customer groups.

Analyzing customer lifetime value requires combining multiple aspects of purchasing behavior. We might join customer information with transaction history, calculate average purchase amounts, and look at shopping frequency over time. This provides insights similar to knowing which customers consistently support your business year after year, but with precise numerical values.

Purchase sequence analysis helps understand customer journeys. Using window functions and self joins, we can examine how customer buying patterns evolve over time. This might reveal that customers often start with entry level products before moving to premium options, similar to observing how a customer's preferences mature over repeated visits.

Churn analysis helps identify customers who might be drifting away. By looking at gaps between purchases and changes in buying patterns, we can spot potential churn before it happens. This is like noticing when a regular customer starts visiting less frequently, but with the advantage of systematic tracking and early warning capabilities.

Promotional impact analysis measures how special offers affect buying behavior. Using before and after comparisons with controlled groups, we can evaluate promotion effectiveness. This resembles observing how a sale sign in the window affects foot traffic, but with precise measurement of results across large customer populations.

Customer feedback analysis often involves working with both structured and unstructured data. While numerical ratings can be easily aggregated, analyzing comment text requires string functions and possibly integration with specialized text analysis tools. This provides insights similar to listening to customer feedback at the counter, but at scale.

Geographic analysis of customer behavior helps understand regional preferences and patterns. By joining customer location data with transaction records, we can identify geographic trends and opportunities. This is like knowing which neighborhoods your customers come from, but with the ability to analyze patterns across entire cities or regions.

Price sensitivity analysis examines how changes in pricing affect purchase decisions. Through careful analysis of sales volumes at different price points, we can understand elasticity of demand for different products and customer segments. This provides more systematic insights than casual observation of how price changes affect sales.

Product affinity analysis identifies relationships between different items in your catalog. Using conditional probability calculations through SQL, we can find products that are frequently purchased together or in sequence. This helps with merchandising decisions and recommendation systems, similar to knowing which products to display together in a store.

Time to repeat purchase analysis helps understand product consumption patterns. By calculating the typical interval between purchases of the same item, we can better predict when customers might need to restock. This is like remembering when regular customers typically run out of their favorite products, but automated and at scale.

Basket size analysis examines how many items customers typically purchase together. Using aggregations and statistical functions, we can understand typical order sizes and their variation across different customer segments or time periods. This helps with everything from inventory planning to marketing strategies.

The real power of SQL for customer behavior analysis comes from combining these different aspects. By joining customer profiles, transaction histories, product data, and external factors like weather or local events, we can build a comprehensive understanding of what drives customer decisions. This allows businesses to move from intuition based decisions to data driven strategies while maintaining the personal touch that makes customers feel valued.

Remember that while SQL provides powerful tools for analyzing customer behavior, the goal remains the same as that of a thoughtful shopkeeper: understanding and serving customers better. The main difference is scale and precision, allowing businesses to maintain personal level insights across thousands or millions of customer relationships.

47. Inventory Management: Tracking Store Stock

Inventory management with SQL mirrors the way we naturally think about organizing and tracking stock in a physical store. Just as a shopkeeper walks the aisles noting which items need replenishing, SQL helps us systematically monitor and maintain optimal inventory levels across thousands of products.

Let's start with the fundamental task of tracking current stock levels. A basic inventory query typically joins product and inventory tables to show quantities on hand, much like counting items on shelves. We can use simple SELECT statements with WHERE clauses to identify items that have fallen below their reorder points, similar to making a mental note when supplies run low.

Stock movement tracking requires more sophisticated queries that examine both inbound and outbound transactions. By using transaction tables with appropriate date ranges, we can analyze how quickly different products move through the store. This helps identify fast moving items that require frequent reordering versus slow moving stock that ties up storage space and capital.

Seasonal inventory planning benefits from historical analysis. Using date functions and aggregations, we can examine how demand fluctuates throughout the year. This might reveal that winter coats start selling in early fall or that swimming supplies peak in late spring, allowing us to adjust stock levels proactively rather than reactively.

Safety stock calculations require statistical analysis of demand patterns. Using standard deviation functions and window operations, we can determine appropriate buffer stock levels based on historical demand variability and desired service levels. This prevents stockouts while avoiding excessive inventory costs, much like keeping extra popular items on hand during busy seasons.

Vendor management queries help optimize the purchasing process. By analyzing lead times, order quantities, and delivery reliability, we can determine optimal reorder points for each supplier. This might involve joining purchase order history with delivery receipts to track vendor performance and adjust ordering strategies accordingly.

Dead stock identification helps prevent inventory from gathering dust. By examining products with no recent sales or movement, we can identify items that might need promotional attention or clearance pricing. This requires joining sales data with inventory records and using time based comparisons to spot stagnant merchandise.

Stock location tracking becomes crucial in larger warehouses. Using location tables joined with inventory records helps optimize pick paths and ensure efficient storage utilization. This might involve analyzing product dimensions, movement frequency, and storage constraints to determine optimal placement strategies.

Unit cost tracking helps maintain accurate inventory valuation. When dealing with varying purchase prices over time, weighted average cost calculations require careful SQL logic to maintain accurate financial records. This involves tracking both quantities and costs across multiple purchase orders and inventory movements.

Inventory reconciliation queries help identify discrepancies between system records and physical counts. By comparing expected quantities with actual counts, we can spot potential issues with theft, damage, or recording errors. This might involve complex joins across receiving, sales, and adjustment records to trace inventory discrepancies to their source.

Product bundling analysis helps manage inventory for items that are sold both individually and as part of sets. This requires tracking component relationships and ensuring adequate stock levels for all possible combinations. It's similar to ensuring you have enough individual ingredients to make complete meal kits.

Expiration date management becomes critical for perishable items. Using date functions and alert queries, we can identify products approaching their sell by dates and prioritize them for sale or use. This helps minimize waste while ensuring product quality and safety.

Cross location inventory management adds another layer of complexity. When managing multiple stores or warehouses, SQL helps optimize stock distribution across locations based on local demand patterns. This might involve analyzing sales velocity by location and facilitating inter store transfers to balance inventory levels.

Reorder point automation requires combining multiple factors into decision logic. Using CASE statements and complex calculations, we can create dynamic reorder points that adjust based on lead time, safety stock requirements, and current demand patterns. This helps maintain optimal stock levels while adapting to changing conditions.

ABC analysis helps prioritize inventory management efforts. By categorizing products based on value and movement frequency, we can focus attention where it matters most. This involves calculating metrics like annual usage value and using percentile functions to assign categories.

The real power of SQL in inventory management comes from its ability to handle complex relationships and large volumes of data systematically. While a skilled shopkeeper might effectively manage a single store's inventory through experience and observation, SQL allows us to apply that same careful attention to detail across vast product catalogs and multiple locations.

Remember that effective inventory management requires balancing multiple competing factors: having enough stock to meet customer demand while minimizing carrying costs, ensuring product freshness while maintaining variety, and optimizing storage space while keeping popular items easily accessible. SQL provides the tools to analyze these tradeoffs systematically and make data driven decisions that keep the business running smoothly.

48. Financial Analysis: Personal Budget Tracking

Financial analysis through SQL brings the same systematic approach to understanding money that we use when managing our personal budgets. Just as we track income and expenses in our daily lives, SQL helps us analyze financial data at scale, revealing patterns and insights that inform better financial decisions.

Let's start with the basics of expense tracking. Much like categorizing our monthly bills, we can use SQL to group and summarize transactions across different expense categories. A simple GROUP BY query with SUM aggregations can quickly show total spending by category, helping identify areas where costs might be running higher than expected. This mirrors how we might review our credit card statement to understand where our money goes each month.

Income analysis requires tracking multiple revenue streams. Just as we might have a regular salary plus side gig earnings, businesses track various income sources. Using date functions and running totals, we can analyze income patterns over time, identifying seasonal trends or growth patterns. Window functions become particularly useful here, allowing us to calculate moving averages and year over year comparisons that reveal longer term trends.

Budget variance analysis helps keep spending on track. By comparing actual expenses against budgeted amounts, we can spot areas needing attention. This involves joining actual transaction tables with budget tables and using CASE statements to highlight significant variances. It's similar to checking our personal budget spreadsheet to see if we're staying within our planned spending limits.

Cash flow projection requires more complex queries that consider timing of both incoming and outgoing payments. Using date based joins and aggregations, we can model expected cash positions over time. This helps anticipate potential shortfalls, much like checking our calendar against upcoming bill due dates to ensure we'll have sufficient funds available.

Profitability analysis by product or service line helps focus efforts on what works best. By joining sales data with cost information, we can calculate margins and contribution amounts. This might involve complex allocations of overhead costs, requiring careful SQL logic to ensure accurate results. It's like analyzing which of our side businesses generates the most profit after accounting for all expenses.

Account reconciliation queries help ensure accuracy of financial records. By comparing transactions across different systems or sources, we can identify discrepancies that need investigation. This might involve matching bank statement entries with internal records, similar to balancing our checkbook but at a much larger scale.

Investment performance tracking requires handling multiple asset types and time periods. Using SQL to calculate returns and risk metrics helps evaluate investment decisions. This involves complex calculations with price data, dividend payments, and currency conversions, much like reviewing our retirement portfolio performance but with more sophisticated metrics.

Accounts receivable aging analysis helps manage cash flow by tracking unpaid invoices. Using date differences and GROUP BY clauses, we can categorize outstanding payments by age and customer. This helps prioritize collection efforts, similar to following up on money owed to us by friends or clients.

Cost allocation across departments or projects often requires sophisticated SQL logic. Using various allocation methods and joining multiple data sources, we can distribute shared costs fairly. This might involve headcount based allocations, usage metrics, or other distribution keys, similar to splitting shared household expenses among roommates but with more complex rules.

Tax reporting preparations benefit from careful SQL analysis. By categorizing transactions according to tax rules and calculating required totals, we can streamline tax compliance. This involves tracking various deductions, exemptions, and special cases, much like organizing our personal tax documents but with greater complexity.

Financial ratio calculations help evaluate business health. Using carefully structured queries, we can calculate metrics like current ratio, debt to equity, or return on assets. This provides quick insights into financial performance, similar to checking our personal debt to income ratio when considering a major purchase.

Forecasting future financial performance requires combining historical trends with forward looking assumptions. Using statistical functions and trend analysis, we can project future results under various scenarios. This helps with planning and decision making, much like estimating how long it will take to save for a down payment based on our current saving rate.

The power of SQL in financial analysis comes from its ability to handle large volumes of transactions while maintaining accuracy and consistency. While we might effectively manage our personal finances with a spreadsheet, SQL provides the tools needed to analyze complex financial relationships across thousands or millions of transactions.

Remember that effective financial analysis requires attention to detail and careful validation of results. Small errors in financial calculations can compound into significant issues, so it's crucial to build in checks and balances. Using SQL's built in features like HAVING clauses and subqueries helps ensure accuracy while maintaining efficiency in our analysis process.

49. Report Generation: Creating Monthly Newsletters

Report generation in SQL transforms raw data into meaningful stories that inform and engage readers, much like crafting a monthly newsletter for family and friends. While a personal newsletter might highlight recent events and milestones, SQL-powered reports systematically organize and present data in ways that reveal insights and drive decisions.

Let's explore how SQL helps create effective reports starting with the basics of data gathering. Just as we might collect family photos and updates for a newsletter, SQL helps us gather relevant information from various database tables. The key is knowing which data elements will best tell our story. A simple SELECT statement forms the foundation, but the art lies in choosing the right columns and joining appropriate tables to create a complete picture.

Data summarization plays a crucial role in report generation. Rather than overwhelming readers with every detail, we use aggregate functions and GROUP BY clauses to present meaningful summaries. This mirrors how we might summarize a month's activities in a newsletter rather than describing every single day. Common aggregations like COUNT, SUM, and AVG help distill large datasets into digestible insights.

Formatting results for readability requires careful attention to detail. SQL's string functions help clean and standardize text output, much like editing newsletter content for consistency. CONCAT functions combine related pieces of information, while CASE statements help create conditional formatting that highlights important information. These tools help transform raw data into polished, professional looking reports.

Time based reporting often forms the backbone of regular newsletters. SQL's date functions help organize information by relevant time periods, whether it's monthly summaries, year to date totals, or year over year comparisons. This might involve calculating period differences, identifying trends, or highlighting significant changes over time, similar to how we might compare this year's family events with last year's memories.

Creating different views for different audiences parallels how we might customize newsletter content for various family members. SQL views help prepare standardized report templates that can be easily reused and modified. This saves time while ensuring consistency across regular reports, much like having a newsletter template that we update each month.

Dynamic parameters add flexibility to reports, allowing readers to customize their view of the data. Using variables or parameter tables, we can create reports that adjust based on user selections. This is like having interactive newsletter sections where readers can choose which topics to explore in more detail.

Visual appeal matters in reports just as much as in newsletters. While SQL itself doesn't create visualizations, carefully structured queries provide the foundation for charts and graphs. Organizing data in ways that facilitate visualization often requires thoughtful use of window functions and pivot operations to present information in the most useful format.

Error handling becomes crucial in automated report generation. Just as we proofread a newsletter before sending it out, we need to build in checks to validate our report data. This might involve comparing totals across different queries, checking for missing information, or flagging unusual values that warrant investigation.

Scheduling and automation help ensure timely delivery of regular reports. Using SQL within scheduled jobs or stored procedures allows reports to run automatically at specified intervals. This maintains consistency while reducing manual effort, similar to setting up automatic newsletter delivery to our mailing list.

Security considerations play an important role in report distribution. Just as we might limit certain newsletter content to immediate family, SQL security features help control who can access different types of report data. This involves careful management of user permissions and possibly row level security to ensure sensitive information remains protected.

Performance optimization becomes increasingly important as reports grow more complex. Efficient query design, proper indexing, and smart use of temporary tables help ensure reports run quickly even with large datasets. This parallels the need to keep our newsletter production process streamlined as our mailing list grows.

Report archival and historical tracking help maintain a record of past communications. Just as we might keep copies of old newsletters, SQL helps us preserve point in time snapshots of report data. This might involve creating archive tables or using temporal features to track how reported information changes over time.

The true art of report generation lies in telling compelling stories with data. This means not just presenting numbers, but providing context and highlighting meaningful patterns. SQL's analytical functions help identify trends, outliers, and relationships that might otherwise go unnoticed, much like crafting engaging narratives for our newsletter readers.

Remember that effective reports, like good newsletters, require a balance of completeness and clarity. While SQL gives us powerful tools to analyze and present data, the key lies in understanding our audience's needs and delivering information in ways that inform and inspire action. Regular feedback and iteration help refine our reporting approach over time, ensuring our reports remain relevant and valuable to their readers.

50. Time Series Analysis: Tracking Fitness Progress

Time series analysis in SQL helps us track changes and patterns over time, much like monitoring our fitness progress throughout the year. Just as we record daily workouts and measurements to understand our health journey, SQL provides powerful tools for analyzing how data changes across different time periods.

Let's start with the fundamentals of time based data collection. When tracking fitness progress, we might record daily weights, workout durations, heart rates, and other metrics. In SQL, this translates to tables with timestamp columns and corresponding measurements. The key is maintaining consistent data collection intervals and ensuring accurate timestamp recording.

Organizing time series data requires careful consideration of time intervals. Just as we might group workout data by days, weeks, or months to spot trends, SQL's date and time functions help us segment data into meaningful periods. EXTRACT, DATEPART, and similar functions let us group measurements by various time components, from hours to quarters.

Moving averages provide valuable insights into trends while smoothing out daily fluctuations. Like tracking a seven day average weight rather than focusing on daily variations, SQL's window functions help calculate rolling averages over specified time periods. This helps distinguish meaningful trends from normal day to day variations in our measurements.

Seasonal patterns often emerge in time series data. Just as we might notice our exercise routines change with the seasons, SQL helps identify recurring patterns in our data. By comparing similar time periods across different years or months, we can understand how cyclical factors influence our measurements. This might involve using modulo operations or periodic functions to identify and analyze seasonal components.

Growth and rate of change calculations reveal how quickly metrics are changing. Similar to tracking how our running speed improves over time, SQL's lag and lead functions help compare values across consecutive periods. This allows us to calculate period over period changes, percentage improvements, and compound growth rates.

Anomaly detection becomes important when monitoring time series data. Just like noticing unusual spikes in heart rate during workouts, SQL helps identify outliers in our time series. This might involve comparing values to historical averages, calculating standard deviations, or using more sophisticated statistical methods to flag unusual patterns.

Forecasting future values based on historical trends helps set realistic goals. While SQL itself isn't a predictive modeling tool, it can help prepare data for forecasting by calculating moving averages, identifying trends, and creating lagged variables. This mirrors how we might project future fitness improvements based on past progress.

Missing data handling requires special attention in time series analysis. Just as we might miss recording some workout sessions, our time series data may have gaps. SQL provides various strategies for dealing with missing values, from simple interpolation to more sophisticated gap filling techniques using window functions.

Comparing multiple related time series helps understand relationships between different metrics. Like analyzing how changes in workout intensity relate to changes in recovery time, SQL helps us align and compare different time series. This might involve self joins, cross correlations, or more complex analytical functions.

Aggregating time series data at different granularities provides multiple perspectives on our progress. Similar to viewing fitness data by day, week, and month simultaneously, SQL's hierarchical time grouping helps us understand patterns at various time scales. This often involves creating summary tables or using ROLLUP and CUBE operations.

Performance considerations become crucial when dealing with large time series datasets. Just as we might summarize older fitness data while keeping detailed recent records, SQL provides techniques for managing historical data efficiently. This might involve partitioning tables by time periods or archiving older data to maintain query performance.

Visualization preparation forms an important part of time series analysis. While SQL focuses on data manipulation, organizing results in ways that facilitate effective visualization is crucial. This might involve pivoting data, calculating supporting metrics, or preparing summary statistics that help tell the story of our progress over time.

Regular monitoring and alerting helps maintain awareness of important changes. Like setting up notifications for missed workout goals, SQL can help establish monitoring systems that alert us to significant changes or threshold crossings in our time series data. This involves combining time series analysis with conditional logic and possibly external alerting systems.

Remember that effective time series analysis requires consistency in data collection and careful consideration of time related factors. Just as sustainable fitness progress comes from regular, well documented effort, meaningful time series analysis depends on reliable data collection and appropriate analytical techniques. The key is choosing the right time scales and analytical methods to reveal the patterns that matter most for our specific needs.

51. User Management: Organizing Team Permissions

Managing user permissions in a database is much like organizing access levels for a team project or running a membership-based organization. Just as you might have different roles like administrators, managers, and regular members in a club, databases need clear structures for controlling who can access and modify different types of information.

Let's start with the fundamental concepts of database users and roles. Think of database roles like positions in an organization - each comes with specific responsibilities and access privileges. Just as a gym might have front desk staff who can check in members but can't modify membership plans, database users can be granted specific permissions that align with their job functions.

Creating users in SQL follows a straightforward pattern. First, we create the user account, then assign appropriate permissions. This is similar to setting up email accounts for new employees and determining which folders and documents they can access. The basic syntax involves CREATE USER statements followed by GRANT commands to assign specific privileges.

Role-based access control provides a scalable way to manage permissions. Instead of assigning permissions individually to each user, we create roles that bundle common sets of permissions together. This is like creating standard permission packages for different job titles - all accounting team members might need the same access levels, so we create an "accounting" role rather than configuring each accountant's permissions separately.

Permissions in SQL can be incredibly granular. We can control access at the server level, database level, schema level, table level, and even column level. This granularity allows us to implement the principle of least privilege - giving users exactly the access they need and nothing more. It's like having different keys for different rooms in a building, ensuring people can only enter areas relevant to their work.

Regular permission audits help maintain security and compliance. Just as organizations periodically review who has access to different systems, database administrators should regularly review user permissions. SQL provides various system views and commands to inspect current permissions, making it easier to identify and correct any access control issues.

Temporary access management requires special consideration. Sometimes we need to grant temporary permissions for specific projects or substitute roles. SQL allows us to grant permissions with time limits or create temporary roles that automatically expire. This is similar to providing temporary badges to contractors or substitute teachers.

Managing group permissions efficiently often involves using schemas. Schemas are like departments in an organization - they help organize related objects and simplify permission management. Instead of setting permissions on individual tables, we can grant access to entire schemas, making it easier to maintain consistent access controls across related data sets.

Revoking permissions requires careful attention to detail. When team members change roles or leave the organization, their access needs to be appropriately modified or removed. SQL's REVOKE commands help us remove specific permissions while maintaining system integrity. This process should be part of a broader off-boarding workflow.

Inheritance and permission hierarchies help streamline access management. Just as department managers might automatically get all the permissions of their team members plus additional privileges, SQL allows us to create hierarchical permission structures. This helps maintain consistent access patterns while reducing administrative overhead.

Monitoring and logging access patterns helps identify potential security issues. SQL servers can track who accesses what data and when, similar to building access logs or system audit trails. This information proves invaluable for troubleshooting, security investigations, and compliance reporting.

Dynamic permission management becomes important in larger organizations. As teams grow and change, permission needs evolve. SQL allows us to create dynamic role assignments based on organizational rules or conditions. This might involve stored procedures that automatically adjust permissions based on user attributes or business rules.

Emergency access procedures need careful planning. Sometimes administrators need to temporarily elevate privileges to resolve urgent issues. SQL provides mechanisms for managing these situations while maintaining security and accountability. This might include special roles for emergency access or procedures for temporary privilege elevation.

Documentation of permission structures is crucial for long-term maintenance. Just as organizations maintain org charts and access control policies, database administrators should maintain clear documentation of user roles, permissions, and the reasoning behind access control decisions. This helps ensure consistent application of security policies and simplifies troubleshooting.

Remember that effective user management balances security with usability. Too restrictive permissions can hinder productivity, while overly permissive access creates security risks. The key is finding the right balance for your organization's needs while maintaining clear documentation and regular review processes.

52. Data Quality: Maintaining Address Accuracy

Data quality is much like maintaining an accurate address book. Just as you want to ensure your holiday cards reach the right destinations, businesses need their customer information to be accurate, consistent, and reliable. Poor data quality can lead to missed opportunities, wasted resources, and frustrated customers, much like how an outdated address book can result in returned mail and lost connections.

Let's explore how SQL helps maintain data quality through various techniques and best practices. Think of data validation as your first line of defense, similar to double checking an address before sending an important package. SQL provides several ways to enforce data quality at the point of entry, including constraints, check conditions, and trigger mechanisms that verify data meets specific criteria before it's saved.

Data consistency is particularly important when dealing with addresses. Consider how the same street might be written multiple ways: "Main Street," "Main St.," or "Main St". Without standardization, searching and analyzing this data becomes challenging. SQL offers string functions and update procedures that help standardize data formats. For example, we can create functions that convert address components into consistent formats, ensuring "STREET" and "St." are all stored the same way.

Here's where data cleansing comes into play. Just as you might periodically go through your address book to update outdated information, databases need regular cleaning. SQL provides powerful tools for identifying and correcting common data quality issues. We can write queries to find duplicate records, detect invalid formats, and identify missing or incomplete information.

Regular data audits help maintain quality over time. Consider creating queries that check for common problems like invalid postal codes, missing apartment numbers, or inconsistent state abbreviations. These audits can be automated to run regularly, flagging potential issues before they cause problems downstream.

Data enrichment processes help fill gaps and verify accuracy. Sometimes we need to supplement our existing data with additional information, like adding ZIP+4 codes or validating addresses against postal databases. SQL can help manage these enrichment processes through update operations and external data integration.

Here's a practical example of data quality management in SQL:

```sql
—Create a procedure to standardize address formats
CREATE PROCEDURE StandardizeAddresses AS
BEGIN
UPDATE Addresses
SET
StreetAddress = UPPER(StreetAddress),
City = INITCAP(City),
State = UPPER(State),
PostalCode = TRIM(PostalCode)
WHERE
StreetAddress IS NOT NULL;
END;
```

Maintaining referential integrity is another crucial aspect of data quality. Just as you might cross reference addresses with a master contact list, databases need to ensure related data stays synchronized. SQL's foreign key constraints help maintain these relationships, preventing orphaned records and maintaining data consistency across tables.

Data profiling helps understand the current state of your data quality. SQL queries can analyze patterns, distributions, and anomalies in your data. This might include checking the percentage of complete versus incomplete addresses, identifying unusual patterns in postal codes, or finding addresses that don't match expected formats.

Time dimension adds another layer of complexity to data quality. Addresses change over time as people move, streets get renamed, or postal codes are updated. SQL's temporal features help track these changes, maintaining both current and historical address information when needed.

Error handling becomes particularly important in data quality management. When invalid data is detected, we need appropriate responses - whether that's rejecting the data, logging the issue for review, or applying automatic corrections. SQL's error handling capabilities help manage these scenarios gracefully.

Performance considerations shouldn't be overlooked when implementing data quality measures. Just as you might organize your address book for quick lookup, database indexes and efficient query design help maintain good performance while ensuring data quality. This might include strategically placing indexes on frequently validated columns or optimizing validation procedures.

Documentation plays a vital role in maintaining data quality standards. Clear documentation of data quality rules, validation procedures, and cleaning processes helps ensure consistent application of standards across the organization. This documentation should include both technical details and business rules that drive data quality requirements.

Regular monitoring helps identify trends and potential issues before they become serious problems. SQL queries can track data quality metrics over time, helping identify areas needing attention or improvement. This might include monitoring error rates, validation failures, or the percentage of records meeting quality standards.

Data quality isn't just about technical accuracy - it's about business value. Poor quality data can lead to missed deliveries, frustrated customers, and wasted marketing efforts. SQL helps maintain data quality through various techniques, but the key is understanding your specific business needs and implementing appropriate validation and maintenance procedures.

Remember that data quality is an ongoing process, not a one time project. Regular maintenance, consistent validation, and continuous monitoring help ensure your data remains accurate and reliable over time. Just as you periodically update your address book, database quality requires regular attention and care to maintain its value to the organization.

The most successful data quality initiatives combine technical solutions with clear business processes. SQL provides the tools, but organizations need to establish clear standards, responsibilities, and procedures for maintaining data quality over time. This might include regular training, clear documentation, and established procedures for handling quality issues when they arise.

53. Batch Processing: Automating Bill Payments

Batch processing in SQL is like setting up automatic bill payments - it's a way to handle many similar tasks efficiently without manual intervention. Just as you might set up recurring payments for your monthly utilities, rent, and subscriptions, batch processing allows databases to handle large volumes of repetitive tasks automatically and reliably.

Think about how you handle your monthly bills. Rather than logging into each account separately to make payments, you likely have a system that automatically processes them on schedule. Similarly, batch processing in SQL automates routine database operations that need to happen regularly and predictably.

Let's explore how batch processing works in practice. Consider a typical billing system that needs to process thousands of customer payments each month. Instead of processing each transaction individually, which would be time consuming and error prone, we can create a batch process that handles them all at once. This might involve several steps: identifying due payments, calculating amounts, applying payments, and generating confirmation records.

The key to effective batch processing is proper organization and error handling. Just as you wouldn't want your automatic bill payments to drain your account if something unexpected happens, batch processes need careful controls and safeguards. This includes checking for sufficient resources, validating data, and maintaining detailed logs of all operations.

Transaction management becomes particularly important in batch processing. Think of it like making sure all your bill payments either complete successfully or don't happen at all - you don't want partial or incomplete transactions. SQL provides transaction control mechanisms that ensure batch operations maintain data integrity, even when processing thousands or millions of records.

Here's where stored procedures come into play. These are like the preset rules you establish for your automatic payments. They contain the logic for handling various scenarios, including what to do when errors occur. A batch processing stored procedure might look something like this:

```sql
CREATE PROCEDURE ProcessMonthlyPayments AS
BEGIN
DECLARE @BatchID int
SET @BatchID = NEXT VALUE FOR BatchSequence
BEGIN TRY
BEGIN TRANSACTION
INSERT INTO PaymentLog (BatchID, PaymentDate, Amount)
SELECT @BatchID, GETDATE(), Amount
FROM PendingPayments
WHERE DueDate <= GETDATE()
UPDATE CustomerAccounts
SET Balance = Balance - Payment.Amount
FROM CustomerAccounts
JOIN PendingPayments Payment
ON CustomerAccounts.CustomerID = Payment.CustomerID
WHERE Payment.DueDate <= GETDATE()
DELETE FROM PendingPayments
WHERE DueDate <= GETDATE()
COMMIT TRANSACTION
END TRY
BEGIN CATCH
ROLLBACK TRANSACTION
INSERT INTO ErrorLog VALUES (@BatchID,
ERROR_MESSAGE())
```

```
END CATCH
END
```

Scheduling becomes an important consideration in batch processing. Just as you might schedule your bill payments for specific dates to align with your paycheck, database batch jobs need careful timing. This might mean running during off peak hours, coordinating with other system processes, or aligning with business cycles.

Performance optimization is crucial for batch processing. Consider how your bank processes millions of transactions each night - the system needs to be efficient to complete everything within the available time window. This might involve techniques like bulk operations, optimized indexes, and careful resource management to ensure smooth processing of large data volumes.

Monitoring and logging help track the progress and success of batch operations. Just as you might review your bank statement to verify all payments processed correctly, batch processes need detailed audit trails. This includes logging start and end times, recording the number of records processed, and maintaining detailed error information when problems occur.

Error recovery procedures are essential for robust batch processing. What happens if a power outage occurs halfway through processing? Just as your bill payment system needs to handle failed payments gracefully, batch processes need clear procedures for handling interruptions and ensuring data consistency.

Parallel processing can improve efficiency for large batch operations. Think of it like having multiple people helping to stuff envelopes for a large mailing - dividing the work can make it go faster. SQL provides various techniques for parallel processing, allowing large batch operations to utilize multiple processors or servers effectively.

Resource management becomes critical when dealing with batch processes. Just as you need to ensure sufficient funds in your account before bills are paid, batch processes need to manage database resources carefully. This might include managing memory usage, controlling disk I/O, and coordinating with other system processes.

Testing batch processes thoroughly before deployment is crucial. This includes testing with realistic data volumes, verifying error handling procedures, and ensuring the system can handle various edge cases. Just as you might do a trial run with a new bill payment service, batch processes need careful validation before being put into production.

Documentation helps maintain and troubleshoot batch processes over time. This includes details about scheduling, dependencies, error handling procedures, and recovery processes. Clear documentation ensures that operations can continue smoothly even as team members change or systems evolve.

Remember that batch processing is about more than just automation - it's about reliable, efficient handling of large scale operations. Whether processing payments, generating reports, or updating records, well designed batch processes help organizations manage their data operations effectively and reliably.

54. API Integration: Connecting Different Services

Imagine trying to get your smart home devices to work together - your thermostat adjusting based on your calendar, your grocery list automatically updating when you run out of items, your music playing as soon as you arrive home. This interconnected system is similar to API integration in SQL, where different services and systems need to communicate and share data seamlessly.

API integration in SQL is about creating bridges between different systems and services, allowing them to exchange information efficiently. Just as your smart home hub needs to understand commands from various devices, a database system often needs to communicate with external services through their APIs (Application Programming Interfaces).

Let's consider a practical example of an online store that needs to integrate with multiple services. The store's database might need to connect with a payment processor for transactions, a shipping service for delivery tracking, and an inventory management system for stock updates. Each of these services has its own API with specific requirements for communication.

SQL plays a crucial role in managing these integrations. When an order comes in through your e-commerce platform, your database needs to coordinate several API calls: checking inventory levels, processing the payment, creating shipping labels, and updating order status. This requires storing and managing API-related data effectively.

Here's how you might structure a basic system for handling API interactions. First, you'll need tables to store API configurations, credentials, and request logs. Think of this like keeping a secure directory of all your smart home device passwords and settings. You might create tables to track API endpoints, authentication tokens, and response histories.

Error handling becomes particularly important when dealing with APIs. External services can be unavailable, respond slowly, or return unexpected data. Your SQL system needs to handle these situations gracefully, much like how your smart home system should handle internet outages or device malfunctions without crashing completely.

Data transformation is another critical aspect of API integration. Different systems often use different data formats and structures. Your SQL system might need to convert dates between time zones, transform currency values, or restructure data to match each system's requirements. This is similar to how your smart home hub might need to translate commands between different device protocols.

Security considerations are paramount in API integration. You need to safely store and manage API credentials, encrypt sensitive data, and ensure secure communications. This is like having a secure system for managing access to your home automation system while preventing unauthorized access to your personal information.

Performance optimization becomes crucial when dealing with multiple API calls. You might need to implement caching strategies, manage rate limits, and optimize the sequence of operations. Consider how your smart home system might batch multiple commands together to reduce network traffic and improve response times.

Let's look at a practical example of handling API responses in SQL. When your system receives data from an external API, you might need to parse and store it efficiently:

```sql
CREATE TABLE APIResponses (
ResponseID int PRIMARY KEY,
APIEndpoint varchar(255),
ResponseData json,
ResponseTime datetime,
```

```
Status varchar(50)
)
CREATE PROCEDURE ProcessAPIResponse
@EndpointURL varchar(255),
@ResponseData json
AS
BEGIN
INSERT INTO APIResponses (APIEndpoint, ResponseData, ResponseTime, Status)
VALUES (@EndpointURL, @ResponseData, GETDATE(), 'Received')
—Process the response based on endpoint type
IF @EndpointURL LIKE '%/payment%'
EXEC ProcessPaymentResponse @ResponseData
ELSE IF @EndpointURL LIKE '%/shipping%'
EXEC ProcessShippingResponse @ResponseData
END
```

Monitoring and logging API interactions helps maintain system reliability. You need to track successful and failed requests, response times, and error patterns. This information helps identify and resolve issues quickly, just as smart home systems log device status and connectivity issues for troubleshooting.

Asynchronous processing often becomes necessary when dealing with APIs. Some operations might take time to complete, and you don't want your system to freeze while waiting for responses. This is similar to how your smart home system might queue up commands when multiple devices need updating.

Version management is another important consideration. APIs can change over time, and your system needs to handle these changes gracefully. This might involve maintaining multiple versions of integration code or implementing feature flags to control functionality.

Testing API integrations thoroughly is crucial. This includes testing normal operations, error conditions, and edge cases. You need to verify that your system handles timeouts, retries, and partial failures appropriately. Consider creating a test environment that simulates various API responses and conditions.

Documentation becomes especially important with API integrations. You need to maintain clear records of API endpoints, authentication methods, data formats, and error handling procedures. This helps other developers understand and maintain the system over time.

Finally, remember that API integration is an ongoing process. APIs evolve, requirements change, and new services need to be integrated. Building a flexible, maintainable system that can adapt to these changes is key to long-term success. Just as smart home technology continues to evolve, your API integration strategy needs to accommodate growth and change over time.

55. Mobile Data: Managing On-the-Go Information

Managing data on mobile devices presents unique challenges and opportunities that differ from traditional database systems. Think about how you use your smartphone - checking messages while waiting in line, updating your shopping list at the store, or tracking your run in the park. Mobile data management needs to handle these on-the-go scenarios while dealing with limited connectivity, battery life constraints, and varying screen sizes.

Mobile databases need to be lightweight yet powerful enough to handle essential operations offline. Consider how your favorite shopping app lets you browse products even without an internet connection, or how your fitness tracker continues recording your workout data during a hike in an area with no cell service. This requires smart synchronization strategies and efficient local storage.

Local data storage on mobile devices works similarly to traditional databases but must be optimized for mobile constraints. Instead of storing large amounts of data, mobile databases often keep only the most relevant information locally while maintaining access to fuller datasets on remote servers. This is like carrying a small notebook with your most important notes while keeping your complete reference library at home.

Synchronization becomes a critical aspect of mobile data management. When you update your task list on your phone, those changes need to be synchronized with your tablet, laptop, and cloud storage. SQL databases for mobile applications need to handle these sync operations efficiently, managing potential conflicts and ensuring data consistency across devices.

Let's look at how you might structure a basic mobile database for a task management app:

```sql
CREATE TABLE Tasks (
TaskID INTEGER PRIMARY KEY,
Title TEXT NOT NULL,
Description TEXT,
DueDate DATETIME,
Priority INTEGER,
SyncStatus TEXT,
LastModified TIMESTAMP,
LastSynced TIMESTAMP
);
CREATE TABLE SyncLog (
LogID INTEGER PRIMARY KEY,
EntityType TEXT,
EntityID INTEGER,
ChangeType TEXT,
SyncStatus TEXT,
Timestamp TIMESTAMP
);
```

Data compression becomes particularly important in mobile environments. You need to minimize the amount of data transferred between devices and servers while maintaining data integrity. This might involve strategies like sending only changed records, using efficient data formats, and implementing smart caching mechanisms.

Battery life considerations affect how we handle database operations on mobile devices. Frequent sync operations can drain battery power quickly, so we need to implement intelligent syncing strategies. This might mean batching updates, scheduling sync operations during charging times, or adjusting sync frequency based on data priority.

Error handling takes on new importance in mobile environments. Network connections can be unreliable, and operations might be interrupted when users switch between apps or receive phone calls. Your database system needs to handle these interruptions gracefully, maintaining data integrity and user experience.

Security presents unique challenges in mobile environments. Mobile devices are more likely to be lost or stolen, so data encryption becomes crucial. You need to implement secure authentication methods and possibly remote data wiping capabilities while ensuring users can still access their data conveniently.

Performance optimization requires special attention on mobile devices. Query operations need to be efficient to conserve battery life and provide smooth user experience. This might involve implementing intelligent indexing strategies, minimizing complex joins, and optimizing data access patterns for mobile use cases.

Offline capabilities are essential for mobile applications. Users expect their apps to work regardless of network connectivity. This requires implementing local storage solutions that can handle basic CRUD operations offline and synchronize changes when connectivity is restored:

```sql
CREATE PROCEDURE HandleOfflineOperation
@OperationType TEXT,
@EntityID INTEGER,
@Data TEXT
AS
BEGIN
INSERT INTO OfflineQueue (
OperationType,
EntityID,
Data,
Timestamp,
```

```
Status
)
VALUES (
@OperationType,
@EntityID,
@Data,
CURRENT_TIMESTAMP,
'Pending'
);
—Update local data immediately
IF @OperationType = 'UPDATE'
UPDATE Tasks
SET SyncStatus = 'Pending'
WHERE TaskID = @EntityID;
END
```

Version management becomes more complex with mobile databases. Different devices might run different versions of your application, requiring careful handling of schema updates and data migrations. You need to implement robust upgrade paths that work reliably even with intermittent connectivity.

User experience considerations often drive mobile database design decisions. Response times need to be nearly instantaneous, even when working with offline data. This might require implementing sophisticated caching strategies and predictive data loading based on user behavior patterns.

Data conflicts require special attention in mobile environments. When multiple devices modify the same data while offline, you need strategies for resolving these conflicts when connectivity is restored. This might involve timestamp-based resolution, user prompts, or sophisticated merge algorithms.

Mobile databases often need to integrate with device-specific features like location services, cameras, and sensors. This requires designing your database schema to accommodate these additional data types and handling the increased data volume they might generate.

Regular maintenance operations need to be handled differently on mobile devices. Database cleanup, optimization, and backup operations need to work within mobile constraints, possibly running only when the device is charging and connected to WiFi.

The future of mobile data management continues to evolve with new technologies like edge computing and 5G networks. Database designs need to be flexible enough to adapt to these changes while maintaining backward compatibility with existing systems and providing consistent user experiences across all devices.

56. Cloud Databases: Storing Family Photos Online

Cloud databases have revolutionized how we store and access our digital memories, much like how photo albums evolved from physical books to online galleries. When you store family photos in the cloud, you're essentially using a database that's accessible from anywhere with an internet connection, offering both convenience and peace of mind.

Think about how families used to store their photographs. Physical albums took up shelf space, could be damaged by water or fire, and sharing meant either making copies or passing around the original album. Cloud databases solve these traditional problems while creating new possibilities for organizing and sharing our memories.

The foundation of cloud photo storage starts with a proper database structure. We need tables to store not just the images themselves, but also important metadata like when and where photos were taken, who's in them, and how they're organized. Here's how we might structure a basic cloud photo storage system:

```sql
CREATE TABLE Photos (
PhotoID INTEGER PRIMARY KEY,
FileName VARCHAR(255),
UploadDate DATETIME,
TakenDate DATETIME,
Location VARCHAR(255),
FileSize INTEGER,
Resolution VARCHAR(50),
StoragePath VARCHAR(500),
UserID INTEGER
);
```

```
CREATE TABLE Albums (
AlbumID INTEGER PRIMARY KEY,
AlbumName VARCHAR(255),
CreationDate DATETIME,
Description TEXT,
UserID INTEGER
);
CREATE TABLE PhotoAlbums (
PhotoID INTEGER,
AlbumID INTEGER,
AddedDate DATETIME,
FOREIGN KEY (PhotoID) REFERENCES Photos(PhotoID),
FOREIGN KEY (AlbumID) REFERENCES Albums(AlbumID)
);
```

When working with cloud databases for photo storage, we need to consider several unique aspects that differ from traditional database applications. One crucial consideration is handling large binary files efficiently. While the actual image files are typically stored in specialized blob storage systems, our database needs to maintain references to these files and manage their metadata effectively.

Security becomes paramount when storing personal family photos in the cloud. We need to implement proper access controls and encryption. This might involve creating sophisticated permission systems that allow sharing specific albums with certain family members while keeping other photos private:

```sql
CREATE TABLE SharePermissions (
PermissionID INTEGER PRIMARY KEY,
AlbumID INTEGER,
SharedWithUserID INTEGER,
PermissionLevel VARCHAR(50),
```

```
ExpiryDate DATETIME,
FOREIGN KEY (AlbumID) REFERENCES Albums(AlbumID)
);
```

Performance optimization takes on new importance in cloud environments. When family members access photos from different locations and devices, we need to ensure quick response times. This often involves implementing caching strategies and content delivery networks (CDNs) while maintaining data consistency.

Cloud databases must handle concurrent access effectively. Multiple family members might be uploading photos, creating albums, or modifying metadata simultaneously. Our database design needs to handle these concurrent operations while preventing data conflicts:

```sql
CREATE PROCEDURE AddPhotoToAlbum
@PhotoID INTEGER,
@AlbumID INTEGER,
@UserID INTEGER
AS
BEGIN TRANSACTION
DECLARE @HasPermission BIT
SELECT @HasPermission = COUNT(*)
FROM Albums
WHERE AlbumID = @AlbumID
AND (UserID = @UserID OR AlbumID IN (
SELECT AlbumID FROM SharePermissions
WHERE SharedWithUserID = @UserID
AND PermissionLevel = 'Write'
))
IF @HasPermission = 1
BEGIN
INSERT INTO PhotoAlbums (PhotoID, AlbumID, AddedDate)
```

```
VALUES (@PhotoID, @AlbumID, GETDATE())
COMMIT
END
ELSE
BEGIN
ROLLBACK
RAISERROR ('Insufficient permissions', 16, 1)
END
```

Storage optimization becomes crucial when dealing with family photo collections that grow over time. We might implement strategies for storing different resolution versions of images, automatically compressing older photos, or archiving rarely accessed images to lower-cost storage tiers.

Backup and recovery strategies need special attention in cloud environments. While cloud providers typically handle hardware redundancy, we still need to protect against accidental deletions or corruptions. This might involve implementing soft delete functionality and maintaining point-in-time recovery capabilities:

```sql
CREATE TRIGGER PhotoSoftDelete
ON Photos
INSTEAD OF DELETE
AS
BEGIN
UPDATE Photos
SET DeletedDate = GETDATE(),
IsDeleted = 1
WHERE PhotoID IN (SELECT PhotoID FROM deleted)
END
```

Search functionality becomes more important as photo collections grow. Cloud databases need to support efficient querying across various metadata fields, possibly including AI-generated tags, facial recognition data, and location information. This might require implementing specialized indexes and search algorithms.

Data synchronization across devices needs careful consideration. When family members upload photos from different devices, we need to ensure all copies stay in sync while handling potential conflicts. This might involve maintaining version history and implementing merge strategies for conflicting changes.

Cost management becomes an important consideration with cloud databases. As storage needs grow, we need to implement strategies to optimize costs while maintaining performance and accessibility. This might involve implementing tiered storage solutions and automatic archiving policies.

Scalability is another key advantage of cloud databases. As your family photo collection grows, the database can automatically scale to handle increased storage and processing needs. This requires careful design of partition strategies and load balancing mechanisms.

Integration with other services often becomes necessary. Your cloud photo database might need to connect with social media platforms, photo editing applications, or printing services. This requires implementing secure APIs and managing external service connections:

```sql
CREATE PROCEDURE SharePhotoToService
@PhotoID INTEGER,
@ServiceName VARCHAR(50),
@UserID INTEGER
AS
BEGIN
—Verify permissions
```

```
—Generate sharing token
—Log sharing activity
—Return sharing URL
END
```

The future of cloud databases for photo storage continues to evolve with new technologies. Machine learning capabilities might automatically organize photos, identify people, or suggest albums. Virtual reality applications might create new ways to experience family photos, requiring additional database capabilities to support these features.

Managing family photos in cloud databases represents a perfect example of how technology can enhance our daily lives while presenting unique technical challenges. By understanding these challenges and implementing appropriate solutions, we can create systems that not only preserve our precious memories but make them more accessible and enjoyable for everyone.

57. Real-time Analytics: Monitoring Home Energy Use

Real time analytics for home energy usage mirrors how we monitor and respond to our daily electricity consumption. Just as we might check our smart thermostat throughout the day to adjust temperature settings, SQL helps us track, analyze, and optimize our home's energy patterns in real time.

Consider how a modern smart home collects energy data. Every device, from your refrigerator to your washing machine, generates a constant stream of usage information. This continuous flow of data requires a different approach to database design and querying compared to traditional static data analysis.

Let's start by creating a basic structure for collecting real time energy data:

```sql
CREATE TABLE DeviceReadings (
ReadingID BIGINT PRIMARY KEY,
DeviceID INTEGER,
Timestamp DATETIME2,
PowerUsage DECIMAL(10,2),
Voltage DECIMAL(8,2),
Current DECIMAL(8,2),
Temperature DECIMAL(6,2)
);
CREATE TABLE Devices (
DeviceID INTEGER PRIMARY KEY,
DeviceName VARCHAR(100),
Location VARCHAR(50),
MaxPowerRating DECIMAL(10,2),
InstallationDate DATE
```

```
);
```

Real time analytics requires efficient querying of recent data while maintaining historical records. We might want to know the current power usage of each device while also analyzing trends over time. This often involves creating time-based partitions in our data:

```sql
SELECT DeviceName,
AVG(PowerUsage) AS AveragePower,
MAX(PowerUsage) AS PeakPower,
DATEPART(HOUR, Timestamp) AS HourOfDay
FROM DeviceReadings r
JOIN Devices d ON r.DeviceID = d.DeviceID
WHERE Timestamp >= DATEADD(HOUR, -24, GETDATE())
GROUP BY DeviceName, DATEPART(HOUR, Timestamp)
ORDER BY HourOfDay;
```

One crucial aspect of real time energy monitoring is detecting anomalies that might indicate problems or opportunities for optimization. We can use window functions to compare current usage against recent patterns:

```sql
WITH RecentReadings AS (
SELECT DeviceID,
PowerUsage,
Timestamp,
AVG(PowerUsage) OVER (
PARTITION BY DeviceID
ORDER BY Timestamp
ROWS BETWEEN 60 PRECEDING AND 1 PRECEDING
) AS AverageLastHour
```

```
FROM DeviceReadings
WHERE Timestamp >= DATEADD(MINUTE, -65, GETDATE())
)
SELECT d.DeviceName,
r.PowerUsage,
r.AverageLastHour,
CASE
WHEN r.PowerUsage > r.AverageLastHour * 1.5
THEN 'High Usage Alert'
WHEN r.PowerUsage < r.AverageLastHour * 0.5
THEN 'Possible Device Issue'
ELSE 'Normal Operation'
END AS Status
FROM RecentReadings r
JOIN Devices d ON r.DeviceID = d.DeviceID;
```

To optimize energy usage, we often need to identify patterns and make predictions. This might involve calculating moving averages and trend analysis:

```sql
SELECT
DeviceName,
DATEPART(HOUR, Timestamp) AS Hour,
AVG(PowerUsage) AS AveragePower,
LAG(AVG(PowerUsage), 1) OVER (
PARTITION BY DeviceID
ORDER BY DATEPART(HOUR, Timestamp)
) AS PreviousHourAverage,
LEAD(AVG(PowerUsage), 1) OVER (
PARTITION BY DeviceID
ORDER BY DATEPART(HOUR, Timestamp)
```

```
) AS NextHourAverage
FROM DeviceReadings r
JOIN Devices d ON r.DeviceID = d.DeviceID
GROUP BY DeviceName, DeviceID, DATEPART(HOUR, Timestamp);
```

Real time monitoring also requires setting up alerts for various conditions. We might create a stored procedure that checks for specific threshold violations:

```sql
CREATE PROCEDURE CheckEnergyThresholds
AS
BEGIN
WITH CurrentUsage AS (
SELECT DeviceID,
PowerUsage,
Timestamp,
MAX(Timestamp) OVER (PARTITION BY DeviceID) AS LatestReading
FROM DeviceReadings
WHERE Timestamp >= DATEADD(MINUTE, -5, GETDATE())
)
INSERT INTO AlertLog (DeviceID, AlertType, AlertMessage, Timestamp)
SELECT
c.DeviceID,
'High Usage',
'Device exceeding normal power consumption',
GETDATE()
FROM CurrentUsage c
JOIN Devices d ON c.DeviceID = d.DeviceID
```

```
WHERE c.Timestamp = c.LatestReading
AND c.PowerUsage > d.MaxPowerRating * 0.9;
END
```

Performance optimization becomes crucial when dealing with real time data. We need to ensure our queries can handle the constant influx of new readings while maintaining quick response times for analysis:

```sql
CREATE INDEX idx_DeviceReadings_Timestamp
ON DeviceReadings (Timestamp DESC);
CREATE INDEX idx_DeviceReadings_Device_Timestamp
ON DeviceReadings (DeviceID, Timestamp DESC);
```

To manage storage efficiently, we might implement a data retention policy that moves older data to summary tables while maintaining detailed recent data:

```sql
CREATE TABLE HourlyEnergyStats (
StatID BIGINT PRIMARY KEY,
DeviceID INTEGER,
HourStart DATETIME,
AveragePower DECIMAL(10,2),
MinPower DECIMAL(10,2),
MaxPower DECIMAL(10,2),
TotalEnergyUsed DECIMAL(12,2)
);
```

Visualization queries help homeowners understand their energy usage patterns. We might create views that format data for different time periods:

```sql
CREATE VIEW DailyEnergyProfile AS
```

```
SELECT
d.DeviceName,
CONVERT(DATE, r.Timestamp) AS Date,
DATEPART(HOUR, r.Timestamp) AS Hour,
AVG(r.PowerUsage) AS AveragePower,
SUM(r.PowerUsage) / 60.0 AS EnergyKWH,
COUNT(*) AS ReadingCount
FROM DeviceReadings r
JOIN Devices d ON r.DeviceID = d.DeviceID
GROUP BY
d.DeviceName,
CONVERT(DATE, r.Timestamp),
DATEPART(HOUR, r.Timestamp);
```

Real time energy monitoring systems often need to integrate with external services, such as weather data or utility pricing information. This might involve creating procedures to correlate energy usage with external factors:

```sql
CREATE PROCEDURE AnalyzeWeatherImpact
@StartDate DATETIME,
@EndDate DATETIME
AS
BEGIN
SELECT
w.Temperature AS OutsideTemp,
AVG(r.PowerUsage) AS AveragePower,
COUNT(DISTINCT r.DeviceID) AS ActiveDevices
FROM DeviceReadings r
JOIN WeatherData w ON
DATEADD(HOUR, DATEDIFF(HOUR, 0, r.Timestamp), 0)
=
```

```
DATEADD(HOUR, DATEDIFF(HOUR, 0, w.Timestamp), 0)
WHERE r.Timestamp BETWEEN @StartDate AND @EndDate
GROUP BY w.Temperature
ORDER BY w.Temperature;
END
```

Understanding and optimizing home energy usage through real time analytics represents a perfect example of how SQL can help us make smarter decisions about our daily resource consumption. By continuously monitoring and analyzing energy data, we can identify opportunities for conservation, detect potential issues before they become problems, and ultimately reduce both our environmental impact and utility costs.

58. Data Migration: Moving to a New System

Moving between database systems is like relocating to a new home. Just as you need to carefully pack, transport, and unpack your belongings when moving houses, data migration requires methodical planning and execution to ensure all your valuable information arrives safely at its new destination.

Data migration becomes necessary for many reasons. Perhaps your current system has reached its capacity limits, like outgrowing a starter home. Maybe you're upgrading to a more sophisticated database platform that offers better features, similar to moving to a house with modern amenities. Or possibly your organization is consolidating multiple databases, much like combining households.

Let's explore a typical data migration scenario. Imagine we're moving customer data from an older MySQL database to a new PostgreSQL system. The first step is understanding your source data completely. Just as you'd inventory your belongings before a move, we need to catalog our existing data structures:

```sql
SELECT
table_name,
column_name,
data_type,
character_maximum_length
FROM information_schema.columns
WHERE table_schema = 'current_database';
```

Before moving any data, we need to prepare the destination system. This means creating appropriate tables and ensuring data types are compatible. Some data types might need conversion, just as some furniture might need modification to fit in a new space. For example, VARCHAR lengths might differ between systems, or date formats might need adjustment.

One crucial aspect of data migration is maintaining data integrity during the transfer. We can use transactions to ensure data consistency, much like ensuring nothing gets lost during a move:

```sql
BEGIN TRANSACTION;
INSERT INTO new_system.customers
SELECT
customer_id,
TRIM(first_name),
TRIM(last_name),
CASE
WHEN phone_number IS NULL THEN 'UNKNOWN'
ELSE phone_number
END,
email_address,
created_date
FROM old_system.customers;
—Verify record counts match
IF (SELECT COUNT(*) FROM new_system.customers) !=
(SELECT COUNT(*) FROM old_system.customers)
BEGIN
ROLLBACK;
THROW 51000, 'Record count mismatch detected', 1;
END
COMMIT TRANSACTION;
```

Data validation is essential throughout the migration process. Like checking each box as it arrives at your new home, we need to verify that our data has transferred correctly:

```sql
WITH SourceCounts AS (
SELECT
COUNT(*) as total_records,
COUNT(DISTINCT customer_id) as unique_customers,
SUM(CASE WHEN email_address IS NOT NULL THEN 1 ELSE 0 END) as email_count
FROM old_system.customers
),
DestinationCounts AS (
SELECT
COUNT(*) as total_records,
COUNT(DISTINCT customer_id) as unique_customers,
SUM(CASE WHEN email_address IS NOT NULL THEN 1 ELSE 0 END) as email_count
FROM new_system.customers
)
SELECT
s.total_records as source_total,
d.total_records as dest_total,
s.unique_customers as source_unique,
d.unique_customers as dest_unique,
s.email_count as source_emails,
d.email_count as dest_emails
FROM SourceCounts s
CROSS JOIN DestinationCounts d;
```

Large datasets often require batch processing to manage the migration efficiently. Think of this like moving your belongings in multiple trips rather than all at once:

```sql
DECLARE @BatchSize INT = 10000;
```

```
DECLARE @CurrentBatch INT = 0;
WHILE EXISTS (
SELECT 1
FROM old_system.customers
WHERE customer_id > @CurrentBatch
)
BEGIN
INSERT INTO new_system.customers
SELECT TOP (@BatchSize) *
FROM old_system.customers
WHERE customer_id > @CurrentBatch
ORDER BY customer_id;
SET @CurrentBatch = @CurrentBatch + @BatchSize;
END
```

Dependencies between tables must be handled carefully, much like moving items in the correct order when relocating. For example, customer orders can't be migrated before customer records:

```sql
CREATE PROCEDURE MigrateRelatedData
@CustomerID INT
AS
BEGIN
—Migrate customer details
INSERT INTO new_system.customers
SELECT * FROM old_system.customers
WHERE customer_id = @CustomerID;
—Migrate customer orders
INSERT INTO new_system.orders
SELECT * FROM old_system.orders
WHERE customer_id = @CustomerID;
—Migrate order details
```

```
INSERT INTO new_system.order_details
SELECT od.*
FROM old_system.order_details od
JOIN old_system.orders o ON od.order_id = o.order_id
WHERE o.customer_id = @CustomerID;
END
```

Historical data often requires special consideration. Like deciding what to keep when moving houses, you might choose to archive older data differently:

```sql
INSERT INTO new_system.archived_orders
SELECT
o.*,
'Migrated from legacy system' as migration_note,
GETDATE() as archive_date
FROM old_system.orders o
WHERE order_date < DATEADD(YEAR, -5, GETDATE());
```

Post-migration testing is crucial. Just as you'd verify everything works in your new home, you need to ensure all database functionality remains intact:

```sql
—Test data accessibility
SELECT COUNT(*) as recent_orders
FROM new_system.orders
WHERE order_date >= DATEADD(MONTH, -1, GETDATE());
—Test relationships
SELECT
c.customer_name,
COUNT(o.order_id) as order_count,
```

```
SUM(o.order_total) as total_spent
FROM new_system.customers c
LEFT JOIN new_system.orders o ON c.customer_id = o.customer_id
GROUP BY c.customer_name
HAVING COUNT(o.order_id) > 0;
```

Finally, maintain detailed documentation of the migration process. Like keeping a record of where everything is placed in your new home, document all data transformations, mapping decisions, and validation results. This documentation proves invaluable for troubleshooting and future reference.

Data migration might seem daunting, but breaking it down into manageable steps makes it achievable. With careful planning, thorough testing, and proper validation, you can ensure your data arrives safely and accurately in its new home.

59. Testing and Debugging: Finding and Fixing Issues

Chapter 59 focuses on testing and debugging SQL queries, a critical skill that's much like being a detective solving everyday mysteries. Just as you might systematically check why your car won't start or why a recipe didn't turn out right, debugging database queries requires a methodical approach to identify and fix issues.

Let's start with a common scenario: imagine you're running a query to calculate total sales by month, but the numbers don't match what you expect. The first step in debugging is to break down complex queries into smaller, testable pieces. Instead of immediately diving into the full query, we can examine each component:

```sql
SELECT
DATE_TRUNC('month', order_date) as sale_month,
SUM(order_total) as monthly_sales
FROM orders
GROUP BY DATE_TRUNC('month', order_date)
ORDER BY sale_month;
```

If this query returns unexpected results, we can start investigating individual orders to verify our data:

```sql
SELECT order_id, order_date, order_total
FROM orders
WHERE order_date >= '2023-01-01'
ORDER BY order_date
LIMIT 10;
```

One common debugging technique is using PRINT or SELECT statements to inspect intermediate results. Think of this like checking the temperature of a roast at different stages of cooking. For complex calculations, we might add columns to verify our logic:

```sql
SELECT
order_id,
quantity,
unit_price,
quantity * unit_price as calculated_total,
order_total as stored_total,
CASE
WHEN quantity * unit_price != order_total
THEN 'Mismatch'
ELSE 'OK'
END as check_result
FROM order_details
WHERE quantity * unit_price != order_total;
```

Data type issues often cause unexpected behavior. Just as mixing metric and imperial measurements can ruin a recipe, mismatched data types can produce incorrect results. Here's how we might debug a joining issue:

```sql
SELECT
CAST(customer_id as VARCHAR) as customer_id_text,
LENGTH(TRIM(customer_id)) as id_length,
ASCII(LEFT(customer_id, 1)) as first_char_ascii
FROM customers
WHERE customer_id NOT IN (
SELECT customer_id
FROM orders
```

```
)
LIMIT 5;
```

Performance problems require a different debugging approach. Like investigating why your car is running slowly, we need to examine execution plans and timing:

```sql
EXPLAIN ANALYZE
SELECT c.customer_name,
COUNT(o.order_id) as order_count
FROM customers c
LEFT JOIN orders o ON c.customer_id = o.customer_id
GROUP BY c.customer_name;
```

Testing should include edge cases, just as you might test a bridge with extreme weights. Here's how we might check for boundary conditions:

```sql
—Test for zero values
SELECT COUNT(*)
FROM orders
WHERE order_total <= 0;
—Test for future dates
SELECT COUNT(*)
FROM orders
WHERE order_date > CURRENT_DATE;
—Test for missing relationships
SELECT COUNT(*)
FROM order_details od
LEFT JOIN products p ON od.product_id = p.product_id
WHERE p.product_id IS NULL;
```

Error handling is crucial for robust applications. Like having a first aid kit ready, we should prepare for potential issues:

```sql
BEGIN TRY
BEGIN TRANSACTION;
UPDATE inventory
SET quantity = quantity - ordered_amount
FROM inventory i
JOIN order_details od ON i.product_id = od.product_id
WHERE od.order_id = @OrderID;
IF EXISTS (
SELECT 1
FROM inventory
WHERE quantity < 0
)
BEGIN
THROW 50001, 'Insufficient inventory', 1;
END
COMMIT TRANSACTION;
END TRY
BEGIN CATCH
ROLLBACK TRANSACTION;
SELECT
ERROR_NUMBER() as ErrorNumber,
ERROR_MESSAGE() as ErrorMessage;
END CATCH;
```

Debugging concurrent operations requires special attention. Like investigating why multiple cooks in a kitchen might create conflicts, we need to understand transaction isolation:

```sql
SELECT
```

```
session_id,
wait_type,
wait_time,
blocking_session_id
FROM sys.dm_exec_requests
WHERE blocking_session_id IS NOT NULL;
```

Documentation plays a crucial role in debugging. Like keeping a maintenance log for your car, commenting your code and documenting known issues helps future troubleshooting:

```sql
/* This query handles special cases:
1. Null prices are treated as zero
2. Negative quantities are ignored
3. Discontinued products are excluded
Last modified: 2023-12-01
*/
SELECT
product_name,
COALESCE(unit_price, 0) as price,
SUM(CASE
WHEN quantity > 0 THEN quantity
ELSE 0
END) as total_sold
FROM products p
JOIN order_details od ON p.product_id = od.product_id
WHERE p.discontinued = 0
GROUP BY product_name, unit_price;
```

Finally, establishing a testing routine helps prevent issues before they occur. Like regular health check-ups, periodic testing of critical queries ensures system reliability:

```sql
CREATE PROCEDURE TestDataIntegrity
AS
BEGIN
—Test for orphaned records
SELECT 'Orphaned Orders' as test_case,
COUNT(*) as issue_count
FROM orders o
LEFT JOIN customers c ON o.customer_id = c.customer_id
WHERE c.customer_id IS NULL
UNION ALL
—Test for invalid calculations
SELECT 'Invalid Totals' as test_case,
COUNT(*) as issue_count
FROM orders o
JOIN order_details od ON o.order_id = od.order_id
GROUP BY o.order_id, o.order_total
HAVING ABS(o.order_total - SUM(od.quantity * od.unit_price)) > 0.01;
END;
```

Remember, debugging is not just about fixing errors; it's about understanding your data and queries more deeply. Each debugging session is an opportunity to improve your code and prevent future issues. By approaching problems systematically and maintaining good documentation, you can make the debugging process more efficient and effective.

60. Documentation: Creating Recipe Instructions

Chapter 60 explores the essential process of creating clear, comprehensive documentation for your SQL databases and queries, drawing parallels with writing detailed recipe instructions. Just as a well-written recipe ensures consistent, delicious results every time, proper database documentation helps maintain data quality and enables smooth collaboration among team members.

Let's start with documenting database structure, similar to listing ingredients and equipment needed for a recipe. Every table should have clear descriptions of its purpose and relationships:

```sql
COMMENT ON TABLE customers IS 'Contains all customer information including contact details and preferences';
COMMENT ON COLUMN customers.customer_id IS 'Unique identifier for each customer';
COMMENT ON COLUMN customers.email IS 'Primary contact email - used for notifications';
```

Think of table documentation like writing the introduction to a recipe. It should explain the purpose, context, and any special considerations. For a customer management system, you might include information about data sources, update frequency, and key business rules. This documentation helps new team members understand the system quickly, just as recipe notes help new cooks understand important techniques.

Query documentation is like writing step-by-step cooking instructions. Complex queries especially need clear explanations of their logic and purpose. Here's an example of a well-documented query:

```sql
/* Purpose: Calculate customer lifetime value (CLV) by segment
Input: Orders and customer data from the last 24 months
Output: Customer segment and associated revenue metrics
Dependencies:
- Requires up-to-date customer_segments table
- Assumes all prices are in USD
Created by: Sarah Johnson
Last Modified: 2023-12-15
Change History: Added seasonal adjustment factor
*/
WITH customer_revenue AS (
SELECT
customer_id,
SUM(order_total) as total_revenue,
COUNT(order_id) as order_count,
MAX(order_date) as last_order_date
FROM orders
WHERE order_date >= DATEADD(month, -24, CURRENT_DATE)
GROUP BY customer_id
)
SELECT
cs.segment_name,
COUNT(DISTINCT cr.customer_id) as customer_count,
AVG(cr.total_revenue) as avg_customer_value,
SUM(cr.total_revenue) as segment_revenue
FROM customer_revenue cr
JOIN customer_segments cs ON cr.customer_id = cs.customer_id
GROUP BY cs.segment_name;
```

Just as recipes often include variations and substitutions, database documentation should cover alternative scenarios and edge cases. This might include handling missing data, dealing with special cases, or accommodating different business rules:

```sql
/* Special Cases:
1. International customers: Convert currency using exchange_rates table
2. Seasonal products: Apply adjustment factor based on month
3. B2B customers: Apply different discount rules
Error Handling:
- Invalid currency codes default to USD
- Missing exchange rates skip conversion
- Negative values are logged for review
*/
```

Performance considerations should be documented like recipe timing and yield information. This includes expected execution times, resource requirements, and optimization notes:

```sql
/* Performance Notes:
- Query typically processes 1M+ rows in 30 seconds
- Requires minimum 4GB working memory
- Benefits from customer_id and order_date indexes
- Consider partitioning by year for larger datasets
Optimization History:
2023-11-01: Added covering index on orders table
2023-12-05: Implemented parallel processing for large segments
*/
```

Maintenance procedures need documentation like cleaning and storage instructions in a recipe. This includes backup procedures, data archiving rules, and regular maintenance tasks:

```sql
/* Maintenance Schedule:
Daily: Verify data integrity
Weekly: Archive completed orders
Monthly: Update statistics
Quarterly: Review index performance
Archiving Rules:
- Orders older than 24 months move to archive_orders
- Maintain customer history for 7 years
- Keep aggregate metrics indefinitely
*/
```

Data quality rules should be documented like quality checks in a recipe. This includes validation criteria, acceptable ranges, and required relationships:

```sql
/* Data Quality Rules:
- Customer email must be unique and valid format
- Order total must match sum of line items
- Shipping address required for physical products
- Product prices must be positive
Validation Queries:
SELECT customer_id, email
FROM customers
WHERE email NOT LIKE '%_@__%.__%'
OR email IS NULL;
*/
```

Just as recipes often include troubleshooting tips, database documentation should address common issues and their solutions:

```sql
/* Common Issues and Solutions:
1. Slow customer segment updates
- Run in batches of 10000
- Schedule during off-peak hours
2. Missing order totals
- Check order_details for incomplete entries
- Verify currency conversion rates
3. Duplicate customer records
- Use fuzzy matching on name/email
- Review merge procedures
*/
```

Finally, like recipe reviews and notes, maintain a section for user feedback and improvements:

```sql
/* Enhancement Log:
Requested:
- Add customer preference tracking
- Implement real-time segment updates
- Expand currency support
Completed:
2023-10: Added mobile number validation
2023-11: Implemented GDPR compliance features
2023-12: Enhanced reporting capabilities
*/
```

Remember that documentation is a living document that should evolve with your database. Regular reviews and updates ensure it remains relevant and useful, just as recipes are refined over time with experience and feedback. Good documentation reduces errors, speeds up development, and makes system maintenance more manageable for everyone involved.

61. Maintenance and Optimization: Home Organization

Maintaining and optimizing a database system is much like keeping your home organized and running smoothly. Just as you need regular cleaning, decluttering, and organizing to keep your living space functional and efficient, databases require ongoing maintenance to ensure they continue performing at their best.

Let's start with daily maintenance tasks, similar to your basic household chores. Just as you might wash dishes and make beds daily, databases need routine checks for error logs, monitoring of available storage space, and verification that scheduled backups completed successfully. These small but essential tasks prevent bigger problems from developing later.

```sql
SELECT tablename, pg_size_pretty(pg_total_relation_size(schemaname||'.'||tablename)) as size
FROM pg_tables
WHERE schemaname = 'public'
ORDER BY pg_total_relation_size(schemaname||'.'||tablename) DESC;
```

This query helps you monitor table sizes, much like keeping track of which closets are getting too full. When you notice tables growing unusually large, it might be time to archive older data or optimize storage strategies.

Regular optimization involves analyzing query performance, similar to identifying bottlenecks in your daily routine. Just as you might notice that morning traffic makes you late and adjust your schedule accordingly, monitoring slow queries helps identify areas needing improvement:

```sql
SELECT relname as table_name,
n_live_tup as row_count,
n_dead_tup as dead_rows
FROM pg_stat_user_tables
WHERE n_dead_tup > 1000
ORDER BY n_dead_tup DESC;
```

This check identifies tables with many dead rows, similar to finding clothes you no longer wear taking up valuable closet space. Regular cleanup of these dead rows through VACUUM operations keeps your database running efficiently.

Index maintenance is like organizing your kitchen cabinets. Just as you want frequently used items easily accessible, properly maintained indexes ensure commonly accessed data can be retrieved quickly. However, too many indexes, like too many storage containers, can actually slow things down:

```sql
SELECT schemaname, tablename, indexname,
pg_size_pretty(pg_relation_size(schemaname||'.'||indexname::text)) as index_size,
idx_scan as number_of_scans
FROM pg_stat_user_indexes
JOIN pg_indexes ON pg_stat_user_indexes.indexrelname = pg_indexes.indexname
WHERE idx_scan = 0
AND pg_relation_size(schemaname||'.'||indexname::text) > 1000000;
```

This query identifies unused indexes consuming space, similar to finding kitchen gadgets you bought but never use. Removing unnecessary indexes frees up resources and can improve write performance.

Statistics maintenance is like keeping inventory of your pantry. Your database query planner needs up-to-date statistics to make good decisions, just as you need to know what ingredients you have before planning meals:

```sql
ANALYZE customers;
ANALYZE orders;
ANALYZE inventory;
```

Regular statistics updates ensure optimal query execution plans, much like keeping your pantry organized helps you plan meals efficiently.

Partition maintenance resembles seasonal closet organization. Just as you might rotate summer and winter clothes, partitioned tables need regular management to maintain performance:

```sql
CREATE TABLE orders_archive
PARTITION BY RANGE (order_date);
CREATE TABLE orders_2022
PARTITION OF orders_archive
FOR VALUES FROM ('2022-01-01') TO ('2023-01-01');
```

This approach helps manage large datasets efficiently, like having separate storage spaces for different seasons of clothing.

Performance monitoring is similar to tracking household utility usage. Regular checks help identify unusual patterns or potential problems before they become serious issues:

```sql
```

```
SELECT pid, now() - pg_stat_activity.query_start AS duration,
query, state
FROM pg_stat_activity
WHERE state != 'idle'
AND now() - pg_stat_activity.query_start > interval '5 minutes';
```

This helps identify long-running queries that might be causing problems, like spotting a running faucet or an open window affecting your utility bills.

Data quality maintenance is like regular home inspection. Just as you check for leaks or wear and tear, regular data quality checks ensure your information remains accurate and reliable:

```sql
SELECT customer_id, email, phone
FROM customers
WHERE email NOT LIKE '%@%.%'
OR phone NOT SIMILAR TO '[0-9+-() ]+';
```

These checks identify data that doesn't meet your standards, similar to identifying areas of your home needing repair or maintenance.

Storage optimization is like maximizing closet space. Techniques such as proper data type selection and compression can significantly reduce storage needs:

```sql
ALTER TABLE customer_notes
ALTER COLUMN notes TYPE text USING notes::text,
SET STORAGE EXTERNAL;
```

This is similar to using vacuum storage bags to compress bulky items and free up closet space.

Finally, regular security maintenance is like checking your home's locks and security system. Regular permission audits and security updates protect your data:

```sql
SELECT grantee, table_schema, table_name, privilege_type
FROM information_schema.table_privileges
WHERE table_schema = 'public'
ORDER BY grantee, table_name;
```

This helps ensure only authorized users have appropriate access, just as you regularly check who has keys to your home.

Remember that database maintenance, like home organization, works best when done regularly and systematically. Creating a maintenance schedule and sticking to it prevents small issues from becoming major problems. Just as a well-maintained home provides a comfortable and efficient living space, a well-maintained database provides reliable and efficient data access for your applications and users.

62. Advanced Reporting: Creating Annual Reviews

Creating effective annual reviews and reports requires mastering advanced SQL techniques that can transform raw data into meaningful insights. Think of it like compiling a family's yearly photo album - you want to tell the complete story while highlighting the most important moments.

Let's start with creating a comprehensive sales performance report. Rather than just showing total numbers, we'll build layers of analysis that reveal deeper patterns:

```sql
WITH monthly_sales AS (
SELECT date_trunc('month', sale_date) as month,
sum(amount) as revenue,
count(*) as transactions,
count(distinct customer_id) as unique_customers
FROM sales
GROUP BY date_trunc('month', sale_date)
),
growth_calc AS (
SELECT month, revenue,
lag(revenue) over (order by month) as prev_month_revenue,
(revenue - lag(revenue) over (order by month)) /
lag(revenue) over (order by month) * 100 as growth_rate
FROM monthly_sales
)
SELECT month,
revenue,
growth_rate,
```

```
avg(revenue) over (order by month rows between 2 preceding and current row)
as three_month_average
FROM growth_calc;
```

This query creates a sophisticated revenue analysis, similar to tracking your family's spending patterns throughout the year. The three-month moving average smooths out seasonal variations, helping identify true trends.

For customer analysis, we might want to segment our customers based on their engagement and value. This helps identify different groups for targeted marketing:

```sql
WITH customer_metrics AS (
SELECT customer_id,
sum(amount) as total_spent,
count(*) as purchase_count,
max(sale_date) as last_purchase,
current_date - max(sale_date) as days_since_purchase
FROM sales
GROUP BY customer_id
)
SELECT
CASE
WHEN total_spent > 1000 AND days_since_purchase < 90 THEN 'VIP Active'
WHEN total_spent > 1000 AND days_since_purchase >= 90 THEN 'VIP At Risk'
WHEN total_spent <= 1000 AND days_since_purchase < 90 THEN 'Regular Active'
ELSE 'Regular At Risk'
END as customer_segment,
```

```
count(*) as segment_size,
avg(total_spent) as avg_customer_value,
avg(purchase_count) as avg_purchase_frequency
FROM customer_metrics
GROUP BY 1;
```

Product performance analysis requires looking at multiple dimensions simultaneously. This query examines product success across different metrics:

```sql
SELECT p.category,
p.product_name,
sum(s.amount) as revenue,
sum(s.quantity) as units_sold,
sum(s.amount)/sum(s.quantity) as avg_price,
sum(s.amount * (1 - s.cost_ratio)) as gross_profit,
count(distinct s.customer_id) as unique_buyers,
sum(s.amount) / count(distinct s.customer_id) as revenue_per_customer
FROM sales s
JOIN products p ON s.product_id = p.id
GROUP BY p.category, p.product_name
HAVING sum(s.amount) > 10000
ORDER BY sum(s.amount) DESC;
```

Geographic analysis can reveal important regional patterns. This query creates a comprehensive regional performance summary:

```sql
WITH regional_metrics AS (
SELECT r.region_name,
count(distinct s.store_id) as store_count,
sum(s.amount) as revenue,
```

```
sum(s.amount)/count(distinct s.store_id) as revenue_per_store,
count(distinct s.customer_id) as customer_count
FROM sales s
JOIN stores st ON s.store_id = st.id
JOIN regions r ON st.region_id = r.id
GROUP BY r.region_name
)
SELECT region_name,
store_count,
revenue,
revenue_per_store,
customer_count,
percent_rank() over (order by revenue) as revenue_percentile
FROM regional_metrics;
```

Creating effective visualizations often requires preparing data in specific formats. Here's how to generate time-series data for charting:

```sql
SELECT date_trunc('week', sale_date) as week,
category,
sum(amount) as revenue,
sum(sum(amount)) over
(partition by category order by date_trunc('week', sale_date))
as running_total
FROM sales s
JOIN products p ON s.product_id = p.id
GROUP BY date_trunc('week', sale_date), category
ORDER BY category, week;
```

For executive summaries, we often need to combine multiple metrics into a single view:

```sql
```

```
WITH metrics AS (
SELECT
extract(year from sale_date) as year,
sum(amount) as total_revenue,
count(distinct customer_id) as total_customers,
sum(amount)/count(distinct customer_id) as revenue_per_customer,
sum(case when is_new_customer then 1 else 0 end) as new_customers,
sum(case when is_repeat_customer then amount else 0 end) /
sum(amount) * 100 as repeat_customer_revenue_percent
FROM sales
GROUP BY extract(year from sale_date)
)
SELECT
year,
total_revenue,
total_customers,
revenue_per_customer,
new_customers,
repeat_customer_revenue_percent,
(total_revenue - lag(total_revenue) over (order by year)) /
lag(total_revenue) over (order by year) * 100 as yoy_growth
FROM metrics
ORDER BY year;
```

Remember that effective annual reports aren't just about numbers - they're about telling a story. Use comments and clear naming conventions to make your queries self-documenting. Consider creating views for frequently used report components:

```sql
CREATE VIEW annual_performance_summary AS
```

```
—Your comprehensive query here
SELECT /* ... */;
```

Finally, always validate your results and include error checking in your reports. Consider adding quality control queries that flag unusual patterns or potential data issues:

```sql
SELECT date_trunc('day', sale_date) as day,
sum(amount) as daily_total,
avg(sum(amount)) over (order by date_trunc('day', sale_date)
rows between 7 preceding and 1 preceding) as avg_previous_week,
case when sum(amount) > 2 * avg(sum(amount)) over
(order by date_trunc('day', sale_date)
rows between 7 preceding and 1 preceding)
then 'Unusual spike'
else 'Normal'
end as volume_check
FROM sales
GROUP BY date_trunc('day', sale_date)
HAVING sum(amount) > 0;
```

This comprehensive approach to annual reporting provides stakeholders with the insights they need while ensuring data quality and completeness. Just as a well-crafted family photo album tells the story of a year's memories, these reports tell the story of your organization's performance and progress.

63. Final Project: Building a Complete System

Building a complete system requires bringing together everything we've learned about SQL into a cohesive whole. Think of it like constructing a house - you need a solid foundation, carefully planned rooms, and all the finishing touches working together harmoniously. In this final project, we'll create a comprehensive event management system that demonstrates how different SQL concepts combine to solve real business needs.

Let's start with the foundation - our database schema. We'll need tables for events, attendees, venues, vendors, and various relationships between them. This schema demonstrates proper normalization while maintaining practical usability:

```sql
CREATE TABLE venues (
venue_id SERIAL PRIMARY KEY,
venue_name VARCHAR(100),
capacity INTEGER,
hourly_rate DECIMAL(10,2),
address TEXT
);
CREATE TABLE events (
event_id SERIAL PRIMARY KEY,
event_name VARCHAR(200),
event_date DATE,
venue_id INTEGER REFERENCES venues(venue_id),
status VARCHAR(50),
budget DECIMAL(12,2)
);
CREATE TABLE attendees (
```

```
attendee_id SERIAL PRIMARY KEY,
first_name VARCHAR(50),
last_name VARCHAR(50),
email VARCHAR(100),
phone VARCHAR(20)
);
```

Our system needs to handle complex relationships, like tracking event registrations, managing vendor assignments, and monitoring payments. These join tables demonstrate how to model many-to-many relationships effectively:

```sql
CREATE TABLE event_registrations (
event_id INTEGER REFERENCES events(event_id),
attendee_id INTEGER REFERENCES attendees(attendee_id),
registration_date TIMESTAMP DEFAULT
CURRENT_TIMESTAMP,
ticket_type VARCHAR(50),
amount_paid DECIMAL(10,2),
PRIMARY KEY (event_id, attendee_id)
);
```

Now let's create some views that will make common operations easier. These views encapsulate complex logic while keeping our application code clean:

```sql
CREATE VIEW upcoming_events AS
SELECT
e.event_name,
e.event_date,
v.venue_name,
count(er.attendee_id) as registered_attendees,
```

v.capacity - count(er.attendee_id) as remaining_capacity
FROM events e
JOIN venues v ON e.venue_id = v.venue_id
LEFT JOIN event_registrations er ON e.event_id = er.event_id
WHERE e.event_date >= CURRENT_DATE
GROUP BY e.event_id, e.event_name, e.event_date, v.venue_name, v.capacity;
```

For data integrity, we'll implement triggers that automatically maintain audit trails and enforce business rules:

```sql
CREATE TABLE audit_log (
log_id SERIAL PRIMARY KEY,
table_name VARCHAR(50),
action_type VARCHAR(20),
record_id INTEGER,
changed_fields JSONB,
changed_at TIMESTAMP DEFAULT CURRENT_TIMESTAMP,
changed_by VARCHAR(50)
);
CREATE OR REPLACE FUNCTION log_changes()
RETURNS TRIGGER AS $$
BEGIN
INSERT INTO audit_log (table_name, action_type, record_id, changed_fields)
VALUES (TG_TABLE_NAME, TG_OP, NEW.event_id,
CASE WHEN TG_OP = 'UPDATE'
THEN jsonb_build_object('old', row_to_json(OLD), 'new', row_to_json(NEW))
ELSE row_to_json(NEW)::jsonb
END);
```
```

```
RETURN NEW;
END;
$$ LANGUAGE plpgsql;
```

Let's create some stored procedures for common operations that require transaction management:

```sql
CREATE OR REPLACE PROCEDURE register_attendee(
p_event_id INTEGER,
p_attendee_id INTEGER,
p_ticket_type VARCHAR(50),
p_amount DECIMAL
)
LANGUAGE plpgsql
AS $$
BEGIN
—Check capacity
IF (SELECT remaining_capacity FROM upcoming_events
WHERE event_id = p_event_id) <= 0 THEN
RAISE EXCEPTION 'Event is at capacity';
END IF;
—Create registration
INSERT INTO event_registrations
(event_id, attendee_id, ticket_type, amount_paid)
VALUES
(p_event_id, p_attendee_id, p_ticket_type, p_amount);
—Update event statistics
UPDATE events
SET total_registrations = total_registrations + 1
WHERE event_id = p_event_id;
COMMIT;
EXCEPTION
```

```
WHEN OTHERS THEN
ROLLBACK;
RAISE;
END;
$$;
```

For reporting, we'll create a comprehensive dashboard that provides real-time insights:

```sql
WITH event_metrics AS (
SELECT
e.event_id,
e.event_name,
e.event_date,
count(er.attendee_id) as total_registrations,
sum(er.amount_paid) as total_revenue,
v.capacity,
v.hourly_rate *
extract(hour from e.end_time - e.start_time) as venue_cost
FROM events e
JOIN venues v ON e.venue_id = v.venue_id
LEFT JOIN event_registrations er ON e.event_id = er.event_id
GROUP BY e.event_id, e.event_name, e.event_date, v.capacity,
v.hourly_rate, e.start_time, e.end_time
)
SELECT
event_name,
event_date,
total_registrations,
total_revenue,
total_revenue - venue_cost as estimated_profit,
```

```
(total_registrations::float / capacity * 100)::integer as capacity_utilized
FROM event_metrics
WHERE event_date >= CURRENT_DATE - interval '30 days'
ORDER BY event_date;
```

Finally, let's implement some performance optimization techniques:

```sql
CREATE INDEX idx_event_date ON events (event_date);
CREATE INDEX idx_registration_lookup ON event_registrations
(event_id, attendee_id);
CLUSTER events USING idx_event_date;
```

This complete system demonstrates how different SQL concepts work together in a real-world application. From data modeling to performance optimization, from business logic implementation to reporting, each component plays a crucial role in creating a robust and maintainable solution. Remember to document your system thoroughly and include proper error handling throughout. Just as a well-built house needs regular maintenance, your database system will require ongoing monitoring and updates to ensure it continues serving its purpose effectively.

The key to success with a project like this is thinking through the user journeys and ensuring your database design supports them efficiently. Start with the core functionality and gradually add features as needed, always keeping performance and maintainability in mind. Test thoroughly at each stage, and don't forget to implement proper backup and recovery procedures.

64. Putting It All Together: Real-World Applications

Throughout this book, we've explored SQL concepts through familiar real-world scenarios. Now it's time to see how all these pieces fit together in actual business applications. Let's look at how organizations use SQL to solve complex problems and drive decision making.

Consider a retail business managing its operations. The morning begins with inventory management queries that combine SELECT statements with JOINs to check stock levels across multiple stores. These queries might trigger automated reorder notifications when inventory falls below certain thresholds. The same database tracks sales transactions in real time, with INSERT statements recording each purchase while UPDATE statements modify inventory levels accordingly.

Customer relationship management provides another comprehensive example of SQL in action. A telecommunications company might use complex queries to analyze customer behavior patterns. They combine customer profile data, service usage records, and payment history using multiple JOINs. GROUP BY clauses help identify trends in service usage, while window functions track changes in customer behavior over time. This analysis helps predict which customers might be at risk of leaving, allowing the company to take proactive retention measures.

Healthcare organizations demonstrate how SQL handles sensitive data securely. Hospitals use views to control access to patient information, ensuring different staff members see only the data they need. Transaction management becomes crucial when updating patient records, as multiple systems might need to access and modify information simultaneously. Complex joins link patient records with treatment histories, medication databases, and billing information.

Financial institutions rely heavily on SQL for transaction processing and reporting. Banks use triggers to automatically update account balances and maintain transaction logs. They employ stored procedures for common operations like fund transfers, ensuring consistency and security. Regular reconciliation processes use aggregate functions to balance accounts, while complex queries detect unusual patterns that might indicate fraudulent activity.

Manufacturing companies use SQL to optimize their production processes. They track raw material inventory, production schedules, and quality control metrics in related tables. Queries combining this data help managers identify bottlenecks and inefficiencies. Time series analysis helps predict maintenance needs, while subqueries and CTEs help calculate complex metrics like overall equipment effectiveness.

E-commerce platforms demonstrate SQL's role in handling high volume transactions. Every product search combines multiple tables to show available items, prices, reviews, and shipping options. Shopping cart systems use temporary tables to track user selections, while order processing involves complex transaction management to ensure payment processing and inventory updates occur correctly.

Educational institutions showcase how SQL handles complex relationships between data. Student information systems link course registrations, grades, prerequisites, and degree requirements. Scheduling systems use constraints and validation rules to prevent conflicts. Regular grade processing uses aggregate functions and window functions to calculate GPAs and class rankings.

Human resources departments illustrate how SQL manages employee data throughout the employment lifecycle. From initial hiring through career progression and benefits management, multiple related tables track employee information. Regular reports use joins and aggregations to analyze workforce metrics, while payroll processing requires precise transaction management.

Content management systems demonstrate SQL's role in organizing unstructured data. News websites use full text search capabilities to find relevant articles, while metadata tables track categories, tags, and related content. Content scheduling uses date functions and triggers, while user engagement metrics rely on aggregate functions and window functions for trend analysis.

Supply chain management shows how SQL coordinates complex business processes. From purchase orders through shipping and delivery, multiple tables track the movement of goods. Real time queries monitor shipment status, while analytical queries help optimize routing and inventory levels across distribution networks.

These real world applications demonstrate several key principles we've covered. First, most solutions combine multiple SQL features rather than using them in isolation. A simple inventory check might involve joins, aggregations, and conditionals in a single query. Second, data integrity becomes crucial in production systems. Foreign keys, transactions, and error handling prevent data inconsistencies that could disrupt business operations.

Performance optimization takes on new importance in production environments. Indexes must be carefully planned to support common queries without overwhelming update operations. Complex queries often need refactoring to improve efficiency, perhaps using CTEs or temporary tables to break down complicated operations into manageable steps.

Security considerations permeate real world applications. Views and row level security control data access, while audit logs track database changes. Backup and recovery plans ensure business continuity, while encryption protects sensitive data both at rest and in transit.

As you apply SQL in real situations, remember that technical skills are just part of the solution. Understanding business requirements helps you design appropriate database structures and write effective queries. Communication skills help you collaborate with stakeholders and explain your solutions to others.

The examples in this chapter demonstrate that SQL remains fundamental to modern business operations. While new technologies continue to emerge, the ability to efficiently store, retrieve, and analyze structured data remains crucial. The practical, problem solving approach you've learned in this book will serve you well as you apply SQL in real world situations.

Remember that every production system started as a simple solution that grew over time. Don't be intimidated by complex requirements. Break down large problems into smaller pieces, test your solutions thoroughly, and gradually build robust systems that serve real business needs.

Don't miss out!

Visit the website below and you can sign up to receive emails whenever Bryan Pine publishes a new book. There's no charge and no obligation.

https://books2read.com/r/B-A-YFKVC-FZNIF

BOOKS 2 READ

Connecting independent readers to independent writers.

About the Publisher

Northwood Lore Books is an independent imprint dedicated to producing accessible, thought-provoking content through the use of advanced content generation systems. All books published under this imprint are created for educational or entertainment purposes only. Authors listed under this imprint use pen names and are not subject-matter experts. Accordingly, no material should be interpreted as financial, legal, medical, or professional advice. The information provided is general in nature, subject to change, and may not reflect the most current data or guidance. Readers are encouraged to consult official sources or qualified professionals before making decisions based on the content herein.

www.ingramcontent.com/pod-product-compliance
Lightning Source LLC
LaVergne TN
LVHW052258200926
848481LV00002B/402
* 9 7 9 8 2 3 0 0 1 9 7 2 5 *